OUTSMART
NEGATIVE
THINKING

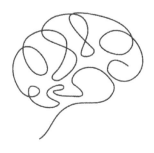

Table of Contents

GIFT

You're going to learn several mindfulness methods in this book to help you bust out of negative thinking and overcome anxiety. While I'm all about gaining knowledge, I'm also about application. It's one thing to intellectually learn these methods and be excited as you're reading but then not implement them into your life.

With application in mind, I've created a downloadable PDF for you. It outlines the mindfulness methods you'll learn in this book. When you're knee-deep in negative thinking and up to your nose in anxiety, the last thing you'll want to do is pick up an entire book, flip through it, and find the section you need. It would be much easier to quickly browse one sheet of paper, identify the mindfulness method you require at that moment and apply it so you can feel happier.

The PDF is minimal, using just enough words to trigger your memory about each mindfulness method so you don't have to spend any more than a few seconds scanning the document to find what you need. To someone who hasn't read the book, the PDF won't make sense or be of use, so don't use the PDF in lieu of reading the book. But to someone who has read the entire book, the PDF document will act as the perfect reminder you need to stay on track and apply the methods discovered here.

Visit
www.nicsaluppo.com/gifts
to get your downloadable gift.

· Introduction

The Life Sucking Nature of Negative Thinking

If you're reading this book, I'm guessing you've experienced having the life sucked out of you by negative thinking and anxiety. I've included both terms in the title, negative thinking and anxiety, because they work together like a 1-2 punch combo. It doesn't matter which comes first—either way, you end up drained and discouraged at best, or severely depressed, even suicidal, at worst. That's why addressing this issue is so important. This is about undergoing a transformation from pain and misery to a life of joy and excitement.

If a negative thought comes first, feelings of anxiety join in soon thereafter. Now, you're in a cycle of negative thoughts fueling anxiety and anxiety fueling more negative thoughts. The same is true if anxiety gets the ball rolling. You might breathe rapidly, feel your heart rate increase, or notice your body tense up, all of which are symptoms of anxiety. From there, negative thoughts *about* the anxious feelings swarm your brain.

This 1-2 combo isn't always debilitating in a traditional sense. When you're sick, you could be laid up in bed for a few days, too weak to do anything. If you break a leg, you probably won't be mountain climbing any time soon. However, with negative thinking, you're more like the walking dead. You get out of bed, feed yourself, and maybe even go to work every day. From the outside, all seems well. But on the inside, there's so much mental and emotional turmoil you don't know if you can make it through even one more day. That's how it was for me.

During the first couple of years suffering from this plight, I was functioning but drained all the time. Negative thinking can zap your energy more than a CrossFit workout. For me, it showed, as I could easily take 3-hour naps due to the sheer mental and emotional stress of having a constant battle raging in my brain.

After a few years, the daily load became too much, and I crumbled. My body looked fine from the outside, but I was breaking down on the inside. Constantly, I was in a negative state, and suicidal thoughts eventually crept in. You'll see what happened next in the section titled "My Journey", coming up in just a few pages.

Let's shine the spotlight on a key insight before moving to the next section—an insight that was true for myself and is true for the clients in my office. It's this: Naturally, you'll try with all your might to address the person, issue, or circumstance you're having negative thoughts or anxious feelings *about*. This is the mistake that keeps you in the life sucking cycle.

If only I could fix the things I'm worrying about and criticizing myself for, life would be peaceful and happy. Not true. My mentor, Ron, who you'll hear about occasionally in this book, said, "The things you're thinking negatively about aren't the problem. The negative thinking itself is the problem." This is huge.

That's what she said. (Fan of *The Office*, anyone?)

I thought I was thinking negatively due to what I perceived as the many awful things happening in my life. However, when an issue or person stopped being problematic, I found *another* reason to think negatively and feel anxious. It was endless. It certainly would have been my doom had I not stopped obsessing over the objects of my negative thoughts and addressed that I could, and would, think negatively about, well, anything. I would find some external person, situation, group, or object to project my internal negativity onto.

To outsmart negative thinking, you'll need to flip your paradigm. Stop thinking that if only you could fix the problem you're obsessing over, then your negative thinking will stop. It won't! You've seen this play out dozens of times because you always find something new to be negative and anxious about. Instead, it's time to think in ways that are helpful and encourage growth. That's the antidote to negative thinking and anxiety: Focusing on ways of thinking which move you towards growth as opposed to thinking in terms of worst-case scenarios and ceaseless self-judgment.

Making the switch from seeing your unhappiness as caused by external circumstances to taking ownership of the fact that you tend towards thinking negatively is the hard part. If you're like

I was, you badly, *desperately*, want to pin the blame on situations rather than on your general approach to thinking. Unfortunately, this is a never-ending battle, as there will always be something new to project your negativity onto. As soon as one problem is solved, your mind will find another to project its negativity onto. There's no way around this—to outsmart negative thinking, you must see it as an internal thinking problem and not an external circumstantial problem.

~ ~ ~

Once you've done the hard part of switching your mindset, it gets easier. The mindfulness methods can be utilized within seconds and with minimal effort. Again, the catch is that you have to believe your unhappiness and struggle are coming from the way you think about circumstances, not the circumstances themselves.

To inspire you, consider a few examples. First, two mountain bikers (MTBers) both break a leg (not the good kind of "breaking a leg") and can't ride for six months. MTBer A focuses on the fact that he can't do what he loves most. Every day, his mind is fixated on the fact that he can't have a biking adventure on the mountain. He's exhausted and miserable. When the six months are over, he's in such a negative place that the prospect of gaining his strength back and redeveloping his skills on the bike is overwhelming and discouraging.

MTBer B focuses his attention on reading a few books that had been on his list for a while. He also creates artwork because it gives him a way to express himself. With the new information in his mind from reading the books plus the creativity flowing through him from doing art, he gets an idea for a website. By the time the six months are over, MTBer B has improved his mind, expressed himself creatively, and implemented a new stream of income on his website. He's excited about the upcoming challenge of building his strength and practicing his technical riding skills.

As another example, consider my own life. You'll hear the details of this later, but for now, know that I live with a challenging physical condition. For years, I thought I'd be happy if the condition would just go away. *It wasn't always this way. Just go back to normal.* It hasn't. Although it may one day, I will not stop enjoying life in the meantime—I'll focus on enjoying what I can do instead of obsessing over what I cannot. However, I didn't always have this mindset.

I had put life on hold for several years, spending my time obsessing and fixating over how badly it sucked that my condition wouldn't get better. Eventually, I realized my physical condition wasn't the source of my misery, the way I was thinking about it was, and I altered my mindset in several key ways:

1. My condition isn't a reason for people to think less of me, it's an easy way of weeding shallow people out of my life.

2. It's not a reason to be an outcast, it's a way to relate more deeply to the pain of others, which isn't always as obvious as my issue.

3. It's not a reason to lose hope for a happy life, it's an opportunity to dig deep into my soul and discover how to have peace *despite* circumstances.

4. It's not a reason to think less of myself, it's a reason to think well of myself for having worked through, and continuing to work through, the associated challenges.

5. It's not something that makes me miserable, it's something that has taught me to face pain head-on instead of avoiding it.

I took something I almost let drive me to suicide and flipped it on its head. My biggest challenge became my best asset. The deepest struggles became what made my life better than it ever was before the condition developed. Not because I changed the condition—because I changed my thinking about it.

Finally, consider Nick Vujicic, who has been a crucial inspiration. Though our problems aren't exactly the same, I reasoned that if Nick V. could be happy and fulfilled with no arms or legs, then Nic S. could live an exciting life with his condition. (That's the first and last time I'll refer to myself in the third person.) Watching his books and videos, his outlook was life-giving, something I desperately needed in my own life.

Nick V. shares his story of being born without limbs and wanting to commit suicide before he was even a teenager. He never transformed into a man with arms and legs, but his outlook about his situation wildly transformed. He stopped fixating on his not having limbs and focused on changing the way he thought about his situation. I didn't know it but what was happening under the surface of my mind as I read *his* story of inner transformation would be the seeds, now 11 years later, which would bloom into this book. Nick was modeling the concept of thinking about your circumstances in a life-giving way as opposed to a soul-draining way, and that was the change I needed to, and did, make.

There's a Method to Thinking

Thinking—there's a method to it. The problem is that 99% of us were never taught how to think. The whirlwind of life was taking place from the time you entered this world, so you learned to spend your time addressing external circumstances, never considering how you think about those circumstances.

In my mid-twenties, I got into fishing because it meant I got to spend time at the lake and play the game of figuring out which lures the fish would go for. When I started, I couldn't figure out how to tie the line to the hook. In my great wisdom, I made a conglomerate knot. You know, the type of knot you loop, swirl, and twist in a thousand directions but, in the end, still comes off the hook. One day, I went fishing with a friend who showed me how to properly tie the knot. Since then, I've taught many others how to tie their hook to the line. Thinking works the same way because you simply need to be taught how to do it.

Thinking well is like having the proper bike to ride down a mountain. . .I'll explain. This summer, we visited Banner Elk, North Carolina. While there, I went to Sugar Mountain, a ski resort that offers downhill mountain biking during the summer months. It's called "downhill" mountain biking because the ski lift carries you to the top of the mountain and you ride your bike back down. Here's the thing—downhill mountain biking is insane. You go over enormous rocks, drops, and steep hills, all of which are far too much for a normal bike to handle.

In getting fitted for a rental bike, I insisted on getting a bike that felt similar to the one I've owned for several years. The young man fitting me for the rental recommended I use a different model, one made for the rocks and drops, but I wanted what felt familiar. I got my way and took the lift up the mountain. After riding down the treacherous terrain one time, it was clear that the bumps and rocks were tossing my rental bike around like it was nothing, as the suspension wasn't heavy-duty enough to take on the rocks and bumps at high speeds. I went back into the shop, saying, "You were right. I need the bike you recommended."

I noticed a difference after just a few seconds on the proper bike, a Giant Glory. It absorbed the bumps with ease. I maintained control riding over rocks that would be crazy to ride over on your average full suspension mountain bike. With the larger suspension system, I could roll over bumps like they were nothing. I couldn't believe how big the boulders and drops were that I was navigating. On the other bike, I surely would have wrecked. But on the Glory, I could maintain stability and control over surprisingly aggressive obstacles.

This book is intended to upgrade the suspension system of your mind. You're going to be able to handle thoughts and situations with ease that formerly knocked your mental stability off its feet. Remember, it wasn't the bumps and rocks on the mountain that were the problem, it was my bike. The resort employee tried telling me, but I wouldn't hear it. I had to experience the bumpy ride for myself before being willing to hear what he had to say.

I hope you've been through enough bumps and wrecks in your life pertaining to negative thinking that you'll be open to the message of this book. Personally, I had to go through a lot of pain before I could hear and apply what I'll be sharing with you. Once I did, though, the ride down the mountain of life became much smoother and way more fun.

What Mindfulness Is

If you're skeptical about the word *mindfulness*, don't worry. While you may think it has to do with wearing a monk's robe while slowly and quietly walking along a dirt path (barefoot, of course), such ideas are stereotypical rather than reality-based. While you certainly can go that route, you can also be mindful while working, driving, interacting with people, at the grocery store, and when an onslaught of negative thinking drops by un-announced.

Mindfulness means this: Pausing to evaluate your thinking, and, if it isn't effective, choosing another mode, method, or style of thinking.

That's it.

The opposite of mindfulness is letting your mind react uncon-sciously, never evaluating whether there's a more effective way to think about people, situations, and challenges.

For this book, we'll need to agree that you can think on two primary levels:

- Experience thoughts while having no sense of evaluat-ing those thoughts.

- Experience thoughts while being aware of them and questioning what you think *about* the thoughts.

As a psychotherapist, I've found one of the most useful ques-tions to ask clients is, "Now that you've shared that, what are your thoughts about it?" Invariably, people will respond, "Well, I see that I did that, but I wish I had done this." Or, "At the time, I didn't realize this, but had I been more present, I would've re-alized it." You have thoughts all day long, but how often do you stop to evaluate the quality and effectiveness of your thoughts? How often do you think about your thinking?

Unless you were raised in a household where you were taught how to think about your thinking, then you'll likely find that your thoughts, when left to their own devices, lean towards judgment, criticism, harshness, and negativity. You'll discover that the methods in this book, when consciously utilized, will create peace and happiness. . .with the keyword here being _utilized_. That is, reading about these methods once won't ingrain them into you, and that's why I created the gift mentioned at the beginning to help you utilize these methods. It will act as a tool you can quickly browse when learning to integrate these new, effective ways of thinking into your life.

My Journey

This section gives you background information regarding how I came to discover and apply the concepts in this book. As you take in my "writing voice" throughout this book, don't think of me as presenting from a podium while wearing a fancy tie as the audience sits nicely in their formal attire. Consider me more like an adventurer who has gotten my own hands dirty hundreds of times. People like letters after names, but I hope you'll give more weight to my "M.A. in Personal Experience" than you will my M.A. in Mental Health Counseling, as many people get their M.A. in Mental Health Counseling without addressing their own personal psychological issues. I'm a fellow journeyman who has a master's degree, not a clinician with head knowledge that hasn't been put to the test in my own life.

With the above in mind, imagine you're about to trek through an unknown forest. As you prepare for your journey, you have access to either someone who has researched and interviewed other people who have trekked the forest but has himself never stepped foot in it, or, someone who has trekked the forest herself dozens of times over. Who do you talk with?

The researcher would say, "At 4.7 miles, you're going to encounter a patch of rocks. My research shows it's easiest to navigate the rocks on the westernmost side. The data proves this, as 77% of subjects who went on the westernmost side were successful, while only 21% of subjects who attempted the easternmost side were successful."

The person who has trekked the forest herself dozens of times over responds to the researcher: "Most people don't know where to grasp the rocks. I didn't know until my fourth time through. The eastern side is certainly more difficult if you don't know where to grasp the rocks. But if you know where to look, then it's much easier than the western side. Let me map out exactly where you need to look so you can easily navigate the rocks on the eastern route."

~ ~ ~

My story pertaining to negative thinking began with experiencing terror and aloneness as a child. It's common that people who think negatively were raised in a dysfunctional household or have experienced an emotionally traumatic event. These

14

experiences lay the foundation for negative thinking to bloom later in life.

Mistakenly, most people think their negative thinking developed because of some experience later in life, such as losing a job, the end of a relationship, or a health issue. This line of thinking makes sense because the negative thoughts become *obvious* after such experiences. However, many people undergo such experiences and remain upbeat and joyful.

The difference is that the people who remain upbeat learned how to think in useful ways about their circumstances. Admittedly, they may have learned how to think unconsciously through the way they were raised or an excellent coach, for example. They didn't know they were learning something so valuable, but they were young enough that the lessons stuck and were naturally applied to challenges later in life.

More importantly, and this is the category I was in and suspect you're in, there are people who make a conscious decision *later* in life to learn ways of thinking to effectively to address life's challenges and stressors.

If someone was fortunate enough to learn to think effectively early in life, they'll naturally carry that into the inevitable challenges life will present. For the majority of us, however, we didn't receive that benefit. The people around us may not have known how to think well about challenges, we had coaches and teachers who treated us poorly instead of uplifting us, and those circumstances laid the foundation for negative thinking to massively bloom during our teen years and into adulthood.

In my own life, I was terrified of my father in addition to playing the role of emotional caretaker for my mother. Being terrified of my father at such a young age, I would not seek comfort from him or go to him with problems. Being the emotional caretaker of my mother, I saw myself as her support pillar as opposed to her being there for me, emotionally speaking, so I would not go to her, either. I had to learn to navigate life without emotional or psychological support by the age of three.

To be clear, my physical needs were well taken care of. There was plenty of food on the table and I even had my own bedroom. We lived in a rural area that afforded the ability to play in the woods and creek daily. We could ride our bikes on the neighbor's smooth driveway and they were not only okay with it, but encouraged it. As long as I stayed busy and active, there were many fun moments. Deep down, however, fear and anxiety were constantly active.

To me, the unhealthy experiences were normal. I thought nothing of my dad being in jail and my mom venting about my dad. I was staying busy and active, so by my estimation, everything was okay. My aunt, whom my parent didn't especially get along with, once visited from California when I was 13. Apparently, she told my mom something seemed off about me in terms of my personality. When my mom told me what my aunt had said, we both laughed. However, after being involved in personal growth starting in my mid-twenties, just 11 years after my aunt's comment, I saw that my aunt was spot on. By the age of 13, when she visited, the foundation for me to be a potentially lifelong negative thinker had already been cemented in. Were it not for having learned and applied the methods in this book, I'd still be thinking negatively today.

When I was young, I couldn't see my negative thinking and anxiety, nor did I want to see them. Sure, I would get so anxious before wrestling matches I could barely function as a kid. In two years of wrestling, I missed 50% of matches due to being "sick." I was sick—not physically, but emotionally and psychologically. And I missed upwards of 30 days each school year, also due to being "sick." At the end of the 6th grade, my English teacher wanted to put me in the advanced course the following year but didn't because, when asked, I told him missing that many days of school was average for me. I was so filled with shame, anxiety, and fear that I wanted to avoid being around my peers.

By the 8th grade, I had fully immersed myself in sports, giving me something to focus my attention on. Were it not for sports, I don't know how I would have coped with life. I like to think I would have gotten into art, music, or another safe outlet, but there's a chance I may have turned to drugs, alcohol, or even suicide. After all, I was considering suicide by my mid-twenties, so that very well could have been me at a younger age had I not stumbled upon sports to keep me distracted from the reality of fear, anxiety, and shame existing deep on the inside.

By 10th grade, missing school was no longer an issue because I had found my identity as an athlete. This carried me through college as well. Great, right? While it lasted, absolutely. However, when someone has completely given their identity over to something that ends when your senior year of college is finished, what is that person to do?

When my last season of track was over, the trauma, depression, fear, shame, and anxiety that had gone unprocessed over the years came rushing back into consciousness like a roaring flood.

It was much worse than during childhood because I had blocked it all out for several years by distracting myself and not dealing with any of it. What came spouting back up was even larger and more intense, psychologically and emotionally speaking, overwhelming me with negativity.

No longer having sports to rely upon plus the addition of a physical condition—a vocal cord issue—which led many people to believe I was drunk or mentally disabled upon hearing my voice, I was utterly enveloped with negative thinking, struggle, and misery daily.

~ ~ ~

How you think can either create happiness and peace or a hell within your own mind and body. I was living in hell. Daily, my thoughts went like this:

- "People think I'm strange and don't want to associate with me."
- "I'm weird."
- "I'm different than everybody else."
- "Nobody understands how I feel."
- "I'm the only one."
- "I'm a loser."
- "I'm inherently 'less than' everyone else."
- "I hate my life."
- "I hate myself."

When you don't know how to think, negative thinking can progress into suicidal ideation. This was the case for me. It had been around three years since my last season as a track athlete, and I was losing hope. Killing myself had become an option in my mind. But the suicidal thoughts weren't completely off the mark. Huh? #Truth. Something about me *did* need to die, but it wasn't my physical body. What needed to die were my old ways of thinking. Not understanding this, I assumed my desire to "die" pertained to my physical self. It wasn't until years later, after having learned and applied the mindfulness methods in this book, that I understood my desire for death was actually healthy, just terribly misdirected to my physical self when it needed to be directed towards my ineffective ways of thinking about life.

In case it's not clear, because it's important that there's no confusion about this, the desire to kill myself was, in reality, a desire to kill off my unhealthy, toxic ways of thinking. Most people don't understand this because they've never considered that they need to learn how to think. You assume your thinking is true and your thoughts are based on reality, never giving your style of thinking much consideration just as you may not consider the water you drink or the air you breathe.

Remember that I wasn't aware of the dynamics being described here. From my perspective, it was all taking place like a whirlwind and I was reacting unconsciously. The beauty of mindfulness is that it places you in the calm eye of the storm, thus stopping the whirlwind of life from toppling you around. From this position, you can consciously choose the most effective ways of responding to your negative thoughts.

The mistake I made was believing my external circumstances were the problem, never considering the real problem was how I thought about and perceived my circumstances. I believed that my voice no longer working as it used to was why I was miserable and considering suicide. *If only it would go back to normal*, I thought, *I'd be happy again.* In my office, I hear this exact line of thinking regularly, but applied to other areas.

If only people wouldn't judge me, I wouldn't be miserable.

If only she didn't say no when I asked her out, I wouldn't be miserable.

If only he would come back, I wouldn't be miserable.

If only I had more money, I wouldn't be miserable.

If only I didn't look the way I do, I wouldn't be miserable.

This type of thinking gives your power away to a circumstance or person, leaving yourself with zero power. Learning to think mindfully *about* circumstances retains 100% of the power for yourself.

My voice is a little better because I've relieved myself of hardcore worrying about it and harshly judging myself for it on a 24/7 basis. Worry and self-judgment will drain your energy and make medical conditions worse due to the stress chemicals they release in your body. You can sit on the couch all day doing nothing, but you'll still be severely exhausted after a day of negative and anxious thoughts. Regarding my voice, although removing the factors of worry and self-judgment created some improvement, it's still an issue in that it's a tough physical effort to speak much of the time. I still get the sideways glances and inappropriate questions. If I ever write a memoir, I'm titling it

What's Up With Your Voice? Personally, socially, and professionally, this is something I have to deal with, and the seven mindfulness methods outlined here allow me to do so with minimal stress.

You've got an idea as to why I sought better, more effective ways of thinking, and we'll dig into the method shortly. First, let's look closely at what, specifically, negative thinking and anxiety are.

What is Negative Thinking?

Stinkin' thinkin'. We know it happens, but what's it made of? For many, it's an ambiguous, undefinable, larger-than-life phenomenon. Luckily, it can be simplified and understood.

To grasp what negative thinking is, you'll first need to know what a thought is, as thinking happens when thoughts are taking place. Thoughts are images or words in your mind. That's it.

When you recall a scene from a show you like, that's a thought. You see images of the scene in your mind's eye. When I see a visual in my mind of the beautiful North Carolina mountains we visited this month, that's a thought. Similarly, when you think of a series of words, such as *I love my new car*, *I want to eat*, or *I'm such a loser*, those are thoughts, too.

If thoughts are words and images in your mind, then *thinking* happens when images and words are actively moving, changing, and flowing through your mind.

With the understanding that thinking takes place when words and images actively flow through your mind, let's address the other part of the phrase—*negative*. This is an ambiguous word. What's meant by this word is something in the lines of, *I'm experiencing unpleasant emotions associated with the thoughts flowing through my mind*.

Surely, if unpleasant emotions weren't present, the thoughts wouldn't be bothersome. They'd be more like a tiny bug buzzing by your ear once and then flying off into the distance. It's the emotion associated with the thought that makes it so "negative." The thought, in and of itself, is neutral. It's the accompanying fear, anger, frustration, anxiety, or sadness that skews a thought from neutral to negative.

People rarely differentiate between thoughts and emotions. Instead, most people unknowingly blend them. Soon, you'll learn how to easily separate the two as well as how to think in ways that prevent you from ending up in a thought-feeling smoothie altogether. (Fruit smoothies = yum. Thought-feeling smoothies = bad for your mental health.)

Let's look at what anxiety is and then jump into the methods.

What is Anxiety?

The anxious brain. Your monkey mind. Anxietizing. Restlessness. *My mind won't shut off.*

Many terms and phrases are associated with anxiety. Much like the term "negative" in *negative thinking*, the terminology surrounding anxiety has become so generalized that it's difficult to succinctly describe it. Let's remove some of the mystery so you can understand what you're dealing with.

You understand that anxiety is uncomfortable. The discomfort is what pushes you to find ways of coping. Tattoos, exercise, and eating are common ways of coping with anxiety, along with alcohol and drug use. I shared a blog post I had written about anxiety on Facebook, and an old high school friend commented, "Just smoke weed every day." That's certainly one way to cope, but wouldn't it be nice to not need weed?

It's a confidence builder to know you don't need weed, tattoos, or alcohol to work through anxiety. Anxiety is so unpleasant that you've been focused on escaping it and, therefore, have given little thought as to what it is. If you're being chased by a monster in a dream, your first reaction will likely be to run. Eventually, when it remains directly on your heels no matter how hard you run and you're too exhausted to continue fleeing or become just plain curious, you'll turn to face the monster. By looking at it directly, you can discover important information to help you defeat it.

Let's take a moment to embrace the discomfort of anxiety—not forever, just for this moment—so you can get an accurate understanding of what it's made of.

~ ~ ~

Anxiety consists of two primary components: The feeling component and the thought component. The feeling component can be interchangeably called the component of emotion.

You know there's an emotional component related to anxiety because physiological sensations go along with experiencing it. That's what all feelings are: physiological. Think of it in terms of feeling a tabletop with your hand, feeling your shirt on your body, feeling you have to use the bathroom in your bladder, and feeling emotions in your body. Emotions are always a physical sensation in your body.

There's also a thought component to anxiety because it involves images or word structures about which you experience fear and worry. For example, if you're anxious about a job interview, you might have images of the interviewer negatively judging you or a series of words run through your mind saying things like,

I'm too dumb,

They won't like me,

or

How could I think I'd have a chance at such a great job?

24

As awful as the above sentences sound, they're merely thoughts. Remember, thoughts consist of a series of words or images running through your mind. The issue is that you may have never considered your negative thoughts to be simply words or images. Instead, you likely identify with them, believe them, and assume they mean something terrible about you.

Since we've established that anxiety has a feeling component and a thinking component, let's combine the two aspects into one easy-to-understand concept that my clients have found to be extremely useful: Anxiety is fear projected into the future.

To exist, anxiety must have an idea of "the future" present. *What's going to happen? Will I be able to handle it when it does happen? Can I continue doing this [in the future]? Can I figure this problem out? Do they think badly of me for what I said last month?* You may have never thought of it this way, but all of those statements are defense mechanisms. That's the purpose anxiety serves—defending against something you don't want to experience in the here and now. Specifically, you project fear into the future to avoid dealing with fear in the now. The seven methods in this book will teach you how to handle fear in the here and now so you don't have to continue living in constant angst.

When you identify what is being defended against and address that issue, the discomfort of the defense mechanism, in this case, anxiety, will dissolve. The larger benefit is you also can address the true issue as opposed to using a defense mechanism. Addressing the true issue instead of peripheral issues is what leads to inner peace. Anxiety will dissolve once the thing it's defending against—fear in the now—is addressed. You'll become

25

confident and comfortable in doing this as you make your way through the mindfulness methods.

As you utilize the methods, your anxiety will dissolve more and more. Regarding the two components of anxiety, the *thought facet* varies from minute to minute, but the *feeling facet* remains consistent in that it's the feeling of fear every single time. To put it succinctly, you have a thought about something, then you project the feeling of fear into the future. That's the stuff anxiety is made of, and you're about to learn to dismantle it.

The purpose of this section was to demystify the concept of anxiety. Simply understanding it consists of various thoughts combined with the feeling of fear projected into the future knocks anxiety off its pedestal of mystery. You *can* heal anxiety and negative thinking by learning different thinking styles in addition to knowing how to handle any associated feelings. It's time to learn how.

The Methods

A Note about the Methods

I prefer writing in a step-by-step manner. Complete Step 1, move to Step 2, and so on. I wrote like that in *Learn to Love Yourself Again* as well as in my first couple of books, which were for athletes. As a former personal trainer, teaching people step-by-step approaches to learning complex exercises such as the power clean was natural. Whereas it took me around eight weeks to learn power cleans, I had the majority of my clients performing them within 1-2 hours. Concepts that require a linear learning model are easy to describe.

With negative thinking, things aren't quite as linear. There are quite literally unlimited manifestations negative thoughts can take. Unlike feelings, of which there are only several, possibilities for thoughts have no end. Your brain can draw from your memory, the environment, other people, the unconscious, the imagined future, and so on.

Don't let this scare you. There may be unlimited options when it comes to negative thinking, but that doesn't mean you're stranded with no way out. It simply requires an approach that is both different and effective. Instead of a linear, step-by-step approach, I suggest keeping an easy-to-reference list of the methods in this book. You can make the list yourself if you prefer, or you can get it premade and ready to go by going back to the "Gift" section at the beginning of this book. When you experience negative thinking, quickly browse the list and choose the best fitting intervention for that moment.

You might use Method #3 twice in a row, then #7 followed by #1 over the course of a day. A month might go by and you've not once used Method #2, but then it becomes just the solution you needed in a particular situation. That's what I mean by this being a non-linear book—you're choosing the method that works best for you in each moment, not using these methods in chronological order.

How do you choose which method to use? It's a lot like picking avocados at the grocery store. Pick one up, squeeze it, and notice its color. You'll choose depending on your need, whether that's to make guacamole dip, spread it on toast, eat it the same day, or eat it a few days from now. From here, this analogy quickly breaks down in a couple of areas. First, some avocados at the grocery store are rotten, but you won't find any rotten methods here—they all serve their purpose in particular situations. Second, there are often 100s of avocados to sort through. Luckily, there are only seven mindfulness methods in this book, so browsing through them all and choosing one takes only a few seconds.

And you'll notice the word "simple" in the subtitle. With each method, there will be stories, examples, and explanations, giving you a solid understanding as to how and why any method operates for your benefit. Then, before moving to the next method, there will be a section called *Simple Application* where I'll distill the method down for you. Note that the simplified version won't make sense unless you've read the complete section. Armed with a complete understanding from having read the entire section, however, the simplified breakdown will allow you to conceptualize the information into an applicable, powerful approach for outsmarting negative thinking without too much information buzzing through your mind.

Before jumping into the methods, you may be wondering, *How do I know if a particular mindfulness method is working?* Simple: You'll be encouraged.

With that in mind, it's time to learn the first mindfulness method.

Mindfulness Method #1

View an Emotion as Just an Emotion

An emotion is just an emotion.

Seems obvious, right? A table is just a table. A shoe is just a shoe. A hat is just a hat. *I'm really nailing this concept.* Not really, though, because there's a difference.

You know a table is just a table. When you sit at a table, you don't freak out. You don't become flooded and overwhelmed. It's just a table. Even if it's got crumbs on top, it's still just a table. With emotions, you haven't applied the same truth.

An emotion is just an emotion isn't something that makes sense (yet) because they can be so. freaking. uncomfortable. . .and scary, and overwhelming, and, well, you get the picture. This is why people drink, use drugs, and seek any other escape route they can find—to avoid emotional discomfort.

In the United States of America, we live under an insane paradigm that goes something like this:

If you're crying, there's something wrong with you. Probably, you need to check yourself into a mental institution or treatment center. If you're afraid, you're weak. If you're angry, you might be tough, maybe, but you're still kind of a psychopath. Unless you're happy and smiling all the time, you've got major problems because you don't fit the mold you're supposed to fit.

This paradigm is completely nuts, but it exists. It's why we have such rampant mental health issues in our society. Feelings themselves are not problematic. The real problem is believing you're not supposed to feel those ways—ever—thus leading to the issue of not processing your feelings. Unprocessed, shoved down feelings create a psychological environment similar to a pond with stagnant water: Bacteria is going to take over.

~ ~ ~

Mindfulness—pausing to become self-aware—will help you notice the driving force behind the urge to escape your feelings. There's a difference between doing something to relax or have fun vs. doing it to escape your emotions.

Taking time to rest, relax, and play after a period of focused work is natural and necessary. It recharges your brain and increases work quality when you come back. But pushing through when your brain needs a break has a diminishing return on the ability to focus and quality of work.

A back and forth between resting and working is natural. But the same activities you use to rest, relax, and have fun can also be an escape from your emotions. I like watching *Parks and Rec*. After writing, optimizing ads, and working with clients during the first half of the day, I'll take a break to eat and put the show on. After getting in some rest and relaxation, I'll write again and then work with a couple more psychotherapy clients.

Similarly, you might like going to the bar and hanging out with your friends to rest and have fun after a long week of work. Both going to the bar and watching TV can be a way of escaping feelings like sadness, fear, or frustration. When done for this purpose, either consciously or unconsciously, the stage for mental illness has been set. This doesn't necessarily mean you'll be mentally ill for a long time, although it's possible.

More common, however, is having a "moment." Saying something you didn't really mean, dropping things, becoming annoyed beyond control at something left on the ground, and so forth. These "moments" are resultant of escaping, instead of processing, your emotions. The deeper your feelings are pushed down, the more they'll affect your well-being and your moments will become more severe.

Escape tactics are anything preventing you from facing and feeling emotions. Exercise, drugs, alcohol, sports, TV, and even religion. I see many people who are highly involved in a religious community desperately struggle with mental illness. There seems to be a belief that prayer, worship, and scripture will take care of the unpleasant emotions. The issue with this mindset is that it further perpetuates avoidance of those emotions. My personal belief is that Christ guides us through the discomfort of such emotions, he doesn't save us from having to experience them.

Counterintuitively, you'll find the only way to escape unpleasant emotions is by welcoming and processing them.

~ ~ ~

I was close to my grandfather. Growing up, he made a true effort to spend quality time with me. Fishing, museums, the local BMX dirt jumps, and playing all kinds of fun games. I trusted him and wasn't afraid of him. He seemed safe. I could relax and be myself around him. This meant the world as I found home life to be terrifying in that I never knew when the next bomb would drop.

When my grandpa died, I was around 30 years old. By then, I'd been on the journey of inner healing for around six years, so I knew repressing my grief wasn't wise. I decided to let myself grieve whenever the urge came up. Of course, I did this within reason. I'm not suggesting you grieve at work during a board meeting. But, if I was alone or with a select few safe people, I made it a point to let it out.

I grieved a lot during the first few months, never believing it meant something was wrong with me. If my body had the urge to let it out, I did. In the next 2.5 years, moments of grief still came up regularly—maybe once every other week or once per month. I kept my commitment to myself and gave the emotions space to "just be," not trying to make them go away.

Six years later, tears sometimes still well up in my eyes when I remember Grandpa Harrington, but it's always with a smile on my face. He was just a normal guy, not famous in the world, but his presence in my life made all the difference. The tears are tears of gratitude and the smile represents fond memories.

Let me make one clarification about my grandpa and grieving his passing. There's a difference between experiencing the pure feeling of grief from the loss vs. experiencing self-pity. Grieving the loss happens when you feel the actual pain of the loss. It hurts to have lost someone, and tears are a way of healing the hurt. But having pity for yourself because that person is gone will be a self-perpetuating cycle. It can go on forever. It avoids having to feel the pain of the loss. With this in mind, as you're grieving, you'll want to ask yourself, *Are these tears expressing the pain of the loss, or are these tears of self-pity?*

The overall point is this: Though my experience of grief surrounding my grandpa's death lasted a few years, it was never burdensome or troublesome. I never experienced it as a problem. Why? I simply let it be as it was. I didn't fight it, battle it, or try to make it go away. What's more troublesome when you have a full bladder: holding it in or letting it flow out?

Grief is simply grief. An emotion is just an emotion. Emotions become problematic when you attach self-critical, self-judgmental thoughts to them. On their own, emotions are neutral. They're simply a bodily sensation. It's the thoughts, usually shameful or self-critical thoughts you unconsciously picked up during childhood, that are the problem. Some emotions may be physically unpleasant; however, that still doesn't mean something is wrong with you for experiencing them.

Back to the bladder example, do you judge yourself when you have to pee? *Oh, I'm so ashamed I have to pee.* That's cray cray talk. You don't judge yourself because it's natural—well, grief, fear, and anger are natural, too. You were taught that they meant something negative about you, which is why you believe an emotion isn't just an emotion.

Now, just like you don't want to be going around urinating on people, there are healthy and unhealthy ways to express your emotions. For instance, anger isn't bad, it's the way you express it that can become harmful. Don't take an "anger dump" on someone. Go in your car, yell into a pillow, or go underwater in a pool and shout. People say, "Joey has an anger problem." No, Joey does not have an anger problem. Joey has a problem with how he expresses his anger. He's taking a dump on your bed instead of into the toilet. That Joey relieved himself is not problematic; the problem is with where and how he relieved himself.

I know the visuals from the previous paragraph weren't so pleasant. I'm hoping to shock you into waking up to the fact that your emotions are not inherently problematic. You're allowed to feel sad, afraid, and angry. Problems arise when:

a) You judge your emotions as meaning something is wrong with you,

   or

b) You express your emotions in a toxic way.

I know I've said it somewhere in the range of three to 1000 times already, but this concept is foundational not only for the rest of this book, but for the rest of your life: The emotions themselves are never the problem.

~ ~ ~

Admittedly, this mindfulness method of viewing an emotion as just an emotion seems counterintuitive. We're supposed to make unpleasant emotions *go away*, not embrace them, right? Mindfulness frees us from the need to do this. Would you rather be free of the need to "run away" from your emotions, or would you rather spend your time endlessly finding more ways to fight against, and avoid, them?

Remember, your emotions are yours, so if you're fighting against them, you're still fighting against yourself. A battle against the self is a fight that can never be won. Even if the dog does bite its own tail, does it really win? If you take time to reflect on this, you'll see that fighting against your feelings has been a source of exhaustion and ongoing frustration in your life.

We can't "make" emotions go away. They're a natural part of life. It was not only morally wrong that someone shamed you for having emotions, but it was also factually inaccurate. Even if you do shove your feelings so far down you don't remember they're there, they'll still drive your life from an unconscious level. Self-sabotage, relationships falling apart one after the other, having difficulty finding your "place" in the world, addictions of all sorts (not just substances), pushing loved ones away, an inability to empathize with others, and being unable to share your truth with others are indicators of being driven by unconscious emotions.

Modern medicine has done its best, but even the leading medicines can only numb trauma and emotional wounds—they can't heal them. A client put it succinctly when he said, "I thought I was healed. But when I got off the medication, all of the same old pain came rushing back immediately. Now, instead of covering up the pain, I want to work through it." And he is. I can't tell you how often this client complained about an inability to handle emotionally intense situations, then came out on the other side saying, "I did it!" Like myself, my colleagues, and my clients, you'll find that the anticipatory fear of emotions is much greater than experiencing them.

~ ~ ~

Again: Fear of emotions is scarier and more intense than actual emotions.

In my mid-twenties, I wanted to get mentally and emotionally healthy. My mentor, Ron, saw that the dynamics I was involved in with my family were, in numerous ways, unhealthy. I didn't get what he was talking about. I thought they were, well, *normal*. When you've always been around something, it seems normal, and you don't experience it as unhealthy.

Since I couldn't see it, Ron recommended I take a 3-month period away from my family. I was terrified thinking about telling them. So terrified, in fact, that it wasn't until a year after he first suggested this that I finally did it. Over that year, he brought it up once every month, but I wasn't ready. Finally, when I was tired of living life the same old ways repeatedly, I planned to tell my family I wouldn't be communicating with them for three months.

To be clear, the point of this wasn't to punish them or get back at them by not talking to them. The point was to remove myself from the toxic interactions long enough to get a sense of, *Oh, this is what life is like without constant toxic family relationships.*

I set a day to go over there and tell them of my plans. I was terrified to look them in the eye and say I wouldn't be in contact for three months. Getting out of my car and walking up to the house, I was physically shaking with anticipatory fear.

Whether a "detox" from the dysfunctional family dynamics you're involved in makes sense to you or not (it didn't make sense to me until after the 3-month period was completed), the point is this: Fear of emotions is scarier than the actual emotions themselves. The anticipation of telling my parents was far scarier than actually telling them.

The point of all of this? Fearing something is not an indicator as to how the experience will play itself out. Most of the time, you're living in negativity and anxiety over something that *might* happen. The odds of a situation playing out in the exact, awful way you're imagining are slim.

As an example, I knew, absolutely *knew*, that telling my parents I would be out of touch for three months would go terribly. I knew it. But what I "knew" and how reality played out were two different things. Although they weren't thrilled and didn't quite understand, there was no explosion or blowout argument.

The issue most people run into regarding *unpleasant emotions such as fear, anxiety, shame, anger, or sadness, is making the feeling mean something about external reality. *This is going to be bad. It's going to be awful. I don't know how I'll get through this.* <u>Beware of the trap of confusing external reality with your internal feelings</u>. Your internal emotions have little to do with external reality. This concept reminds me of a friend riding the Magnum XL-200 for the first time at Cedar Point.

*I hesitate to use the word "unpleasant," as, over the years, I've found holding emotions in to be one hundred times more unpleasant than feeling and expressing them.

We were 13 and the Magnum was the largest roller coaster in the park. It was fairly crowded, and during the one-hour wait to get on the ride, my friend was sweating and shaking. Continuously, he asked questions like, "Are you sure it's not that bad?" "How long does it take?" "Do you think I'll be okay?" He even expressed anger that we had somehow convinced him to try the ride as if him deciding to ride the coaster was all our fault.

Once the ride was over, he was giddy, happy, and excited. He loved it and couldn't stop smiling and raving about how great it was. An emotion is just an emotion. That's it. It doesn't mean anything about external reality. My friend believed the way he felt before getting on the ride meant something about how he would feel during or after the ride, and that belief ended up being wildly bogus.

~ ~ ~

An emotion is just an emotion. You avoid your emotions out of a belief that they mean something's wrong. Instead of feeling them, you might drink, use drugs, watch TV, or stay busy doing something else. If you're reading this book, your drug of choice might be cyclical negative thinking patterns. *I'll think my way out of this* is a way to avoid feeling something. In looking closely, you'll see that while you may think your way out of a particular situation, the same emotions keep coming back again and again in new situations. Then, you've got to think your way out of a new situation. It becomes a daily cycle.

Outsmarting negative thinking means feeling your feelings right here and now as opposed to avoiding them or projecting them into the future. In letting your emotions run their course and live out their life cycle, you'll find that the same emotional patterns don't continue popping up again and again but in new circumstances. Emotions are neutral until you attach a negative meaning to them—be vigilant in reminding yourself that emotions are neutral and have no meaning unless you create it with your mind. Be careful to not assume any meaning your parents or caregivers gave to your emotions was accurate. They may have shamed you for experiencing emotions, but they didn't know any better.

Taking this a step further, I like to attach a positive meaning to uncomfortable emotions. As an example, let's say I'm feeling sadness. Okay, good. It's good because I can get it out of my body, not holding it down. Or, maybe I'm feeling frustrated. Good. It's good because it's an opportunity to let it out in a healthy way, then reevaluate how I'm mentally approaching that specific situation I'm frustrated about. If an intense emotion pops into my awareness, good. It was there all along hanging out somewhere in my psychological makeup, so now this saves me the time of having to go digging for it.

Facing uncomfortable emotions is an opportunity to improve your tolerance of them. We idolize being able to tolerate physical discomfort in our society—think CrossFit workouts, professional athletes, and Navy SEALs—but rarely does anyone discuss the value of making a conscious choice to walk through painful feelings. The first day you go out and run, you'll be breathing heavy, your lungs will be burning, and your calves will feel like battery acid is pumping through them. After running regularly for three months, the same distance from the first day will feel much easier on your body. Your tolerance has improved.

In the same way, when you consciously feel your feelings, your tolerance for intense emotions expands rapidly. This is important, because it removes the need to find ways of escaping your emotions. Avoiding your emotions is a never-ending battle because, as a human being, emotions will always be part of you. Building emotional tolerance, however, will positively affect the rest of your life.

An emotion is just an emotion.

Simple Application

It's important to understand that you unconsciously learned the belief that emotions mean something negative. Since you learned it, you can unlearn it.

When you experience an emotion you find to be unpleasant, remind yourself that it doesn't mean anything about you. Then, give yourself time to sit with that emotion and let it run its life course through you.

One client said, "When I pause and just let myself feel my feelings, I feel better and can move on with the rest of my day in a clear-minded manner. But when I try to avoid or fight them, it becomes an all-day, exhausting event. I'd much rather just take a few minutes to feel them so I can then be free to move on with my day."

Mindfulness Method #2

Know What You're Really Afraid Of

It's all too easy to think you're afraid of one thing and never address the true issue.

I'm afraid of being judged by other people is a common case of thinking you're afraid of one thing when it's really something else. People will spend years, decades, and even a lifetime avoiding judgment from other people, but the real culprit of the fear lies within you, not without.

Let's clarify this concept with an example. I used to think I was afraid of asking girls, and then women, out. Some of my thoughts around this subject were:

- *What if she says no?*
- *What if she rejects me?*
- *What if she laughs at me?*

Among men, this is quite common. Many, many men in the world are interested in dating but don't know how to work through this so-called fear of rejection. As I became more mindful about my thoughts and emotions, the epiphany I needed came to me: I'm not afraid of being rejected, and I'm not afraid of being told no. I'm afraid of how I'll *feel* on the inside if I'm rejected or told no.

Did you get that? The true fear is fear of your own emotions, *not* the external event. You say you're nervous about a job interview. You're not nervous about the job interview, you're nervous about how you will feel as you go through it or when the company informs you of the outcome. You say you're afraid of being judged by people. You're not afraid of being judged, you're afraid of the feelings you'll have if you perceive yourself as being judged. I wasn't afraid of asking women out, I was afraid of how I'd feel on the inside.

Without mindfulness, you can go a lifetime thinking you're afraid of one thing, never addressing the actual fear: Your own feelings.

~ ~ ~

What is one to do with this knowledge? The fear hasn't gone away. After all, you're just more accurately aware of what it's about. Well, that's good, because you can stop blaming outside circumstances. Instead, the true issue can be addressed—the scary, overwhelming emotions you don't know how to productively handle.

Let's work through this together using a common example I hear in my office: *I knew I needed to talk to my partner, but I was just waiting for the right time.*

Notice the above statement is written in the past tense. Yes, sadly, it's often too late. So many people avoid the hard conversations in their relationship, thinking they'll do it when the time is "right," only to have the relationship blow up or their partner end it before the right time arrives.

Of course, waiting for the right time is a fallacy, as it doesn't exist. Actually, I take that back—the right time does exist, just not in the sense you're imaging it. You want the right time to exist in terms of "feeling comfortable" with no anxiety about the conversation. In that sense, the right time will never arrive. However, in another sense, there is such a thing as the right time.

The right time exists when you decide it exists. Here's how that works: It's the right time to have the hard conversation when you are willing to embrace the discomfort. See the difference? In the fallacy version of the "right time," it never exists. In the reality-based version of the right time, it exists when you decide it exists, as it's all up to you. Are you willing to embrace the discomfort?

This applies to dozens, even thousands, of other areas. Add your own if you don't see it on this short list:

- There's not going to be a right time to begin exercising. The right time is whenever you decide you're willing to work through the uncomfortable feelings associated with doing it.

- There's not going to be a right time to try stand-up comedy. The right time is when you decide you're willing to work through the uncomfortable feelings associated with doing it.

- There's not going to be a right time to make amends with your child. The right time is when you decide you're willing to work through the uncomfortable feelings you associate with saying, "I'm sorry" and admitting you did something hurtful.

- There's not going to be a right time to switch career paths. The right time is when you decide you're willing to work through the uncomfortable feelings associated with uncertainty and the unknown.

- There's not going to be a right time to dance. The right time is when you decide you're willing to embrace the uncomfortable feelings associated with dancing. Once you've done that, you'll just start moving. This can be applied literally to dancing, something many people have a fear of, or, "dancing" can be a symbol for living life in general.

You can use the sentence structure above, filling in any particular area you're personally dealing with in your life: There's not going to be a right time to [fill it in here]. The right time is when I decide I'm willing to work through the uncomfortable feelings.

~ ~ ~

In the previous section, there was a lot of talk about embracing uncomfortable emotions. For healing and transformation to take place, this is an essential. Luckily, it's quite simple.

When I say it's simple, I'm not saying it's not scary. Your old paradigm believes anything that's scary is bad and should be avoided. That's the old way. In your new paradigm, scary does not equal difficult, bad, or something to avoid. That's what it *doesn't* equal, but what *does* it equal? In the new paradigm, scary equals the edge of your confidence zone. Given that expanding your confidence zone is a plus, scary things can be exciting, as there's more confidence waiting for you on the other side of experiencing them. Distinguishing between physical danger vs. unpleasant emotions will help tremendously here. We'll break this down using the example from earlier about having an important conversation with your partner.

When you think about having this conversation, your body responds as it would respond if a physical threat were present. Your heart rate increases, nervous system activates, muscles tense in anticipation of fighting or fleeing, and breathing becomes rapid. This is a useful biological mechanism for handling physical threats. However, for handling emotions, it can continuously send you running away from a ghost "out there" when the real issue you need to address is on the inside.

The ghost shows up whenever you so much as think about having the hard conversation with your partner. When your mind is occupied with something such as working, reading, watching a show, listening to a podcast, eating, or sleeping, the ghost is gone. You're no longer nervous about the tough conversation. Where did the threat go?

Consider that all of the listed distractions above (working, TV, etc.) can temporarily relieve emotional threats, but none can make a physical threat go away. If there's a venomous snake in your kitchen, trying to distract yourself with cooking, eating, or a show won't make the threat disappear. No matter how hard you try to watch *The Office*, you'll remain fixated on the snake.

This brings us full circle, back to the concept of embracing fear. By not embracing the uncomfortable emotions, you'll never have the tough conversation with your partner, ask the person you're interested in to have coffee, explore the new career path, or set a boundary with your friend or family member. Given there is no physical threat, the only way to accomplish the thing you want to accomplish—like the examples in the previous sentence—is by walking through the fear and other unpleasant feelings associated with doing those things. While physical threats are wise to avoid, avoiding emotional threats will keep you stuck for a lifetime.

I shared this example in *Healing Your Inner Critic*, but it's so poignant that I'll share a briefer version here. I was on a men's personal growth intensive and we were hiking down a mountain after having climbed up with a professional guide service. There was a large boulder, around 8-ft tall, and I had the urge to stand on top of it and let out a roaring shout.

I said to our group's facilitator, "I want to get on the rock and yell, but I'm scared."

His response was revolutionary. He said, "You can both yell and be scared at the same time."

Until he said that, I thought that being scared meant *don't do that thing.*

I climbed up, feeling scared. I then started yelling, feeling both scared *and* excited to be yelling. Next, I was simply yelling and enjoying the experience. The takeaway is that I had to go through the fear and discomfort to reach the fulfillment and freedom on the other side. There was no physical danger. The only threat was the feeling of fear taking place inside of me.

Notice, and this is very important, that it requires in-the-moment mindfulness to distinguish whether a physical danger is present or whether a threat pertains to your uncomfortable emotions.

A moment ago, I said that this method is simple. It is. It was quite simple to climb atop the rock, open my mouth, and yell. Once I decided to both feel afraid and yell at the same time, there was nothing hard or complicated about it. It only seems hard when you have resistance to feeling fear, anxiety, or another unpleasant emotion. Just like you can do unpleasant activities to grow a business and make money, so too can you experience unpleasant emotions to grow and mature psychologically. Facing uncomfortable feelings is the gateway into doing the things you've longed to do, but haven't done because fear was made into a "reason why not."

~ ~ ~

The reason you think feeling afraid means *don't move forward* even when there's no physical danger present is simple. When you were a kid, you experienced feelings like fear, sadness, and frustration—emotions all children (and adults) experience. If the people you most relied upon shamed you for having such feelings, it meant that showing those feelings was a threat to your ability to survive. Remember, you were a helpless, completely dependent child at the time. As an adult, that's no longer the case, but you still unconsciously hold the belief in your psychological makeup, and that belief drives your decision making for handling uncomfortable feelings.

To clarify, when you were a child and your parents shamed you, let's say, for expressing the feeling of sadness, you couldn't differentiate between psychological abandonment and physical abandonment. Being shamed *is* abandonment, but it's emotional and psychological abandonment, not physical abandonment. Within that experience of being shamed, there's nobody there for you, emotionally speaking. You may still get fed and have a roof over your head, so no physical threat exists, but psychologically, you're alone.

Remember, you need to consider this from the perspective of a small, totally dependent child. Don't mistakenly project what you now understand about the world or your parents onto your 4-year old self. "Well, my dad was just coping with his own problems, and that's why he was constantly yelling, slamming things, and berating me." True, but to a 4-year old, those things are perceived as threats to life itself, and that's how the brain and body of your 4-year old self responded to those things.

From the eyes of a totally dependent child, psychological abandonment is similar to physical abandonment in terms of the level of anxiety present. Remember, this is all happening unconsciously. It's not as if you, as a child, could step back and observe, *Oh, I see what's happening here. My parents are triggered by my feelings because they haven't resolved their own emotional wounds. My sadness reminds them of theirs, and that's too painful for them to feel, which is why they are shutting me down. But my feelings are still okay and natural—it's my parents who need psychological growth and development.*

Your child self wasn't aware enough to see it in that way. All you knew was:

Expressing fear = I get abandoned by my caretakers.

Then, the next time the feeling of fear or sadness came up for you, you stopped yourself, swallowed it, and pretended you were fine. As a child, the acting and pretending saved you from being psychologically abused and abandoned.

Can you now see why, as an adult, you think being afraid means ***do not proceed***, even when there's no physical threat present? It's a very old defense mechanism you unconsciously developed. To be clear, it was necessary for making it through that portion of your life without melting down. However, when this mechanism is still active as an adult, it holds you back from being the type of person you want to be.

Being mindful is the key. Ask, "Am I afraid of this person or situation due to a physical threat, or am I afraid of the feelings I might feel associated with the experience?" If there is a

52

physical threat, act accordingly. Seek safety. Run. Flee. Fight, if you must. However, if no physical threat exists, ask yourself, "Will avoiding this situation bring me closer to the type of life I want to live, or will embracing the uncomfortable feelings and taking action bring me closer to the kind of life I want to live?"

If you decide taking action is the best route to bring you towards the type of person you want to be, then know this:

You can both feel embarrassed *and* dance.

Simple Application

Next time you feel an uncomfortable feeling, pause. In pausing, ask yourself, "Does this situation pose a physical threat? Or, am I afraid of the feelings I'm experiencing?"

If there is a physical threat, take immediate action to keep yourself safe.

However, if there is no physical threat, determine whether the action you're considering will shape you more into the person you'd like to be. If the answer is yes, step toward the discomfort. The primary goal here is to move into the discomfort, whether that means you're nose deep in it or just ankle deep. Either is better than walking the other way. While you're at it, don't forget: An emotion is just an emotion.

Mindfulness Method #3

Evaluate This Moment

Not an hour from now, not yesterday, and not tomorrow. This moment.

After locking up the office yesterday evening, I got into my car, turned it on, and started backing out of the parking space. As I pressed the brakes, I continued moving. I pressed harder. Still nothing, even with the pedal all the way to the floor. I was rolling towards the building.

Throwing it into park was the only option I could think of at the moment, which I'm certain wasn't good for the vehicle, but did stop the car before it smashed into the building.

I'm concerned I'll have to buy a new car. My car is older, and it wouldn't be worth dumping lots of money into repairing it. A new car would be a big stretch right now, financially speaking.

As I stood in the parking lot waiting for my wife to pick me up, various negative thoughts and angst-riddled scenarios circulated through my mind. *Can I afford a new car right now? How many more clients will I have to add to my schedule? I'm going to get burned out because I'll have too many clients and will have to give up writing. I'll never write again. I can't believe I have to give up writing. I hate this. I hate life. Life sucks.*

Whoa, there, Nic's brain—that became a crisis quite fast.

Noticing my thoughts were spiraling into Crazy Town, I paused. That's what mindfulness is all about—pausing. Upon pausing, I asked myself, *Am I okay at this moment?* I answered honestly, *Yes, I am.* As I stood in that parking lot, I became aware of a soft breeze, beautiful trees all around me, and a sense of quiet and peace. At that moment, I was okay.

The following morning: I contacted a mechanic I know who works on Hondas, and he had to cancel this morning due to illness. The car is still stuck in the middle of the lot. Not ideal. But am I okay? Yes.

I'm aware that there's going to be a towing fee, and who knows how much the repairs are going to cost? Could be a couple hundred or could be upwards of 1-2k. *But right now, at this moment, am I okay? Yes.*

~ ~ ~

Sometimes, you're not okay in a moment. In those cases, you need to act by calling someone, asking for help, or doing whatever else is necessary. But, with negative thinking and anxiety,

56

those moments when you're genuinely not okay don't constitute the majority of instances.

The problematic, common moments are those in which you, indeed, are okay right now, but imagine things won't be okay at some point in the future. One common way this happens is replaying something you said or did over and over, imagining it will make things not okay in the near future. In these situations, if you stopped and ask yourself, *Am I okay, right now, at this moment?,* the answer would have to be *yes.* Let's explore two examples.

The *Why Did I Say That?* Example
Everyone is familiar with this, but if you struggle with negative thinking and anxiety, you're especially familiar with it. What I'm referring to is when an interaction has come and gone, but you're obsessing over something you've said or done.

It's so embarrassing, I can't believe I said that. But, at this moment, are you okay? Are you being verbally abused or physically attacked for what you said? That certainly happens, and in those cases, action is necessary. The more likely scenario, however, is that you are okay, but you're feeling embarrassment or shame.

People who are deeply bothered and embarrassed about having said or done something that didn't show themselves in the best light imagine that other people *never* do this. Somehow, you believe that normal, intelligent people never say the wrong thing, stumble over words, make jokes that aren't funny, or do embarrassing things. It's simply not true. The only way to never make a blunder is by living such a rigid and calculated life that you're alive but not really living at all.

If you're saying things to yourself like *I can't believe I did that* or *Why did I say that?* my response to you is: Because you're a human being and human beings sometimes say things that don't make sense, lose their train of thought, or stumble over their words. Instead of beating yourself up, pause and ask yourself, *at this moment, right here and right now, am I okay?*

The *Worrying about An Outcome* Example

This takes place when you project your mind into the future, feeling anxiety about a future situation as if it were happening right now. I experienced this at a company I interned with.

The company lacked leadership, with the owner of the company expressing complaints about the staff via email. Rarely was anyone spoken to in person. The issue was that the owner had specific, high expectations of employees and interns but lacked the ability to a) communicate those expectations and b) provide the support needed for such expectations to be executed.

Every Sunday night was "email night," when the owner would send out a weekly email to the staff. The email was called something like a team update, but it was essentially the owner outlining complaints about the staff week after week and demanding the shortcomings be corrected. When someone isn't taking self-ownership as a leader, as Forest Gump might say, their emails are like a box of chocolates—you never know what you're gonna get.

I remember one particular sequence of emails. The first said, "Our secretary will be leaving. I'll be hiring a new secretary soon." A few days later, an email read, "Each staff member and intern will pick up two hours of secretary duty per day, unpaid." The email contained no ownership or apology over the fact that, just a few days prior, we were told a new secretary would be brought aboard.

It takes just one email like that to lose employee respect, drop morale to zero, and desecrate any pride people had in working for that particular company. Of course, the situation could still have been repaired and respect restored with a follow-up email acknowledging and apologizing for the incongruency, but that never happened. And none of the employees brought it to the owner's attention because they were already looking for new job opportunities. They must have found new jobs, too, because the turnover rate was quite high.

The work environment was a constant struggle between the owner and staff members. Considering the inability of the owner to engage in respectful communication, I was often projecting my mind out into the future. *What's the owner going to say next? Am I going to be the target this time?* I certainly was the target a couple of times, as was everybody else.

I enjoyed the clients I worked with at this company, but the work environment was miserable. Given this was an internship of only six months, I stuck it out, as I needed the internship to graduate with a master's degree. Almost daily, my mind would project into the future about what the owner might do or say next, and I would experience anxiety and negative thoughts as if the situation was taking place now.

In reality, I was at home eating, watching a movie with my wife, or getting ready for bed. Had I stopped to ask, *Am I, at this moment, okay?,* the answer would have been yes. However, I was so caught up in the toxic work environment that I was living in it day and night inside my brain and body. *What if the boss's lid completely flips and I don't graduate? How will I make it through the next few months without the owner singling me out?* Safety, beauty, and peace were all around me, but I created danger by worrying about an outcome in the future.

When you're in the midst of a stressful season in your life, this can be tough. *Will my marriage work out? Will I graduate? Will I find a job? Will my child be okay?* All of these are examples of highly challenging situations. Of course, it's wise to take action and do damage control where you can. But during the other moments, like while you're eating, going for a walk, showering, and so on, pause, asking yourself, *at this moment, am I okay?*

~ ~ ~

Another day has gone by, and I'm still not sure what will become of my car. The mechanic looked at it yesterday. He thinks it's a brake line issue. But that was based on a quick look. It's still in the lot of my office building and won't be towed until Monday. That means I won't have an idea as to the price of the repair until Monday at the earliest, but more likely, Tuesday. As I write this, it's Saturday morning.

This would be a great opportunity to let my mind run wild.

What if it's a $1000.00 repair? Or more? I can't afford that.

If it is more than $1k, surely it wouldn't be worth repairing since the car is so old. I'd be better off getting a new car. But can I afford that? I'm going to be broke. My life will revolve around car payments.

Instead, ever since the brakes gave out Thursday evening, I've been asking: *Am I, right now, at this moment, okay?* The answer has been yes. Every. Single. Time. This very moment, I'm sitting at the kitchen table, and it's early enough in the morning that our neighborhood is quiet. I can hear birds chirping. I'm okay. The only reason I wouldn't be okay at this moment is if I were projecting my mind into a future circumstance of doom and gloom.

I can embrace the peace at this moment, or I can project my mind three days into the future, creating anxiety at this moment. I have options. While there may not be an option as to the outer circumstance that unfolds, I have options as to how I internally handle my thoughts in the here and now.

Simple Application

When you notice your mind running wild over potentially ill-fated, futuristic circumstances, congratulations—you noticed! Noticing is the first step. If mindfulness is about one thing, it's about taking a moment to notice.

Next, determine if, aside from your negative thoughts, you're okay at this moment. It helps to feel your feet on the ground while taking a gentle, slow breath through your nose. The breathing itself does nothing special mentally, but *noticing* the breathing puts you in the NOW. Look at some objects around you. Right now, I'm seeing a stack of books, a wooden desktop, and a wooden cup holder with the shape of a sea turtle at its center. I'm aware of the empty space between myself and the door. It's peaceful.

After you've noticed a few things, ask yourself, "Am I, at this moment, okay?"

Mindfulness Method #4

Face Your Emotional Trauma Head On

Negative thinking and anxiety are often rooted in a vague sense that an awful, terrible outcome will happen in the future. Such a mindset has everything to do with how reality *has* played out and nothing to do with how reality *will* play out.

We often think we're "winning" when we keep busy, put our heads down, and avoid thinking about past painful events. "It's in the past," they say. "Just let it go and move on," is their motto. With an understanding of psychological science, nobody would say such things.

Trauma and emotional wounds stick in your body. Even if you're not thinking about it because you're staying busy, it's still there. Negative thinking and anxiety are symptoms of trauma and emotional wounds. They aren't THE problem, but a natural consequence of unhealed trauma. I'm not going to go through the hard science supporting these truths here, but my book *Trauma: Curative Concepts* addresses it thoroughly, exploring the research conducted by Peter Levine, Bessel van der Kolk, and John Sarno.

Before facing and healing my own psychological trauma, I constantly thought in terms of worst-case scenarios. Every day, and in everything I did, I had a sense that something terrible would happen. Going to work? Something terrible will happen. Going on a date? Something terrible. I was too scared to live life because I viewed my anxiety and negative thinking as gauges of reality instead of the symptoms of unaddressed trauma they were—let that sink in.

People think they're getting the best of their past when they avoid thinking about it. *I don't let it bother me*, you may tell yourself. If it didn't bother you, you'd be able to take a calculated risk, explore options, and generally live life as an adventure. Instead, everything is overanalyzed, causing you to freeze and not move forward with important decisions. As a result, your life stays the same.

I know an intelligent person who works for a nonprofit in Georgia. While he's grateful for his job, he'd like to be doing something else. But in his own mind, he's not good enough. *Nobody would want to hire me*, he tells himself, thus preventing himself from even exploring what's out there. Because he views his thoughts as a gauge of reality, his life is frozen in place and change can't happen.

Trauma has to be stored somewhere. It doesn't just go away by not thinking about it. If you put food in your body, it will need to be processed. Certainly, the phrase *out of sight, out of mind,* makes no sense with food or drink you've ingested. Similarly, you must also process what you've psychologically ingested. If you haven't, you're psychologically bloated.

Maybe you ingested verbal or emotional abuse as a child. You might've lost someone close to you. Your parents may have been physically there but emotionally absent. It could be a health issue that turned your life upside down. You may have been through a gut-wrenching relationship. Whatever it is or whatever it was, these experiences must be processed. Not digesting your food properly leads to stomach issues. Not digesting psychological experiences properly leads to mental and emotional issues. Negative thinking and anxiety are symptoms of unprocessed experiences.

Once you address your emotional wounds, much of what you've been thinking negatively about will vanish. Not because the external situation has changed, but because the way you see the world from the inside out will have changed. As an example, I grew up in an alcoholic and codependent household. One second, I'm having fun with my G.I. Joes, and the next, an explosive argument is happening. It was an unpredictable environment.

Because of the unpredictability, I became an adult who demanded predictability, avoiding most spontaneous or uncontrollable circumstances. *I'm a planner,* I'd tell myself, which is actually code for *I'm afraid of life.* One day, I had a breakthrough. It seems so small now, but back then, it was a huge step. I was going to visit a friend who lived about an hour away. Instead of getting directions before leaving, I started driving there and called him for directions while I was on my way.

Laughing, he said, "What? You're on your way and you don't know how to get here?"

"Yup," I said, not letting on to what a major deal this was for me.

I had woken up, psychologically speaking, around that time, so the decision was made with purpose. I knew it would be a way of breaking out of my need to plan and be in control. I wanted to teach myself that the vague sense of something going terribly wrong existed in my head but not in reality. To clarify, I'm not suggesting you become irresponsible by not making necessary preparations for the various events in your life. I certainly wouldn't have done this if it were a job interview or important meeting. What I am suggesting is this: Prove to yourself you can handle the unknown. You'll find that the thought of the unknown is far scarier than the experience of the unknown.

The changes you long for in life happen in the unknown. Unfortunately, unresolved traumas and emotional wounds create associations of "bad" and "scary" with the unknown. Start small and show yourself you can handle the unknown. You need these experiences to teach yourself that how life *has* played out is not necessarily how it *will* play out. Set some time aside to drive in a random direction and find something fun to do. Speak up at your support meeting without first planning out in your mind every word you'll say. Let someone else handle loading the dishes or folding the towels. "How will it turn out?" you ask. Answer: Unknown. And, that's okay.

There's an organization called the Hero's Journey Foundation, and the entire premise of their yearly intensive is making friends with the unknown. In preparing to attend the intensive for the first time in 2010, my mentor explained that part of the experience involves going into a cave. A cave? I was terrified, imagining being scrunched up in a hole in the ground, not knowing if I'd ever get out. But due to too much rain, our group didn't go into the caves at all—another example of how worrying steals time you can never get back.

The point of The Hero's Journey Foundation is to consciously face the unknown to work through the uncomfortable feelings that arise. One activity involves climbing a telephone pole and then jumping off. Of course, you're harnessed with ropes that catch you before hitting the ground. But you're not jumping into a net or into a foam pit. Let me ask you this: Do you think people are more afraid when climbing the pole in anticipation of the jump or during the actual jump? If you guessed the anticipation portion, you'd be right. Once the jump is taken, fear is gone because there's nothing that can be done. Given that nothing can be done once you're in the air, a sense of letting go and surrender ensues.

After each activity, whether pole jumping, mountain climbing, or giving your own eulogy, you'll discuss your experience with the group. Typically, you'll answer questions like: *How did you feel? What was the fear like? Now that you've made the jump, what do you think of the fear? Do you relate to fear differently now than before you experienced this activity?*

The experiences carry over into daily life. Your body remembers that the unknown doesn't have to equal bad or scary. There's more willingness to experiment and explore, so life opens up as a result.

Knowing that perceiving something as scary, even terrifying, doesn't mean that it's necessarily bad was a life-transforming lesson for me, and it can do the same for you, too. I can't tell you how often I was terrified on the Hero's Journey intensive, but so much good came from saying, *Hello, fear. Shall we accompany one another through this exercise?* That's the difference embracing fear, not running away from it, makes.

Fear is a natural human emotion and there will always be another scary event just on the horizon. Because it's part of life, learning to navigate fear, instead of spending your life avoiding it, makes sense. Knowing how to handle fear is infinitely more valuable than being adept at avoiding situations that are scary. There's never a point in life when the next challenge isn't just around the corner, for example:

- Meeting Santa Clause
- Losing your first tooth
- Having your first goldfish die
- The death of a pet dog
- Going to grade school
- Going to high school
- The snowball dance—will he ask me?
- The snowball dance—will she say yes if I ask her?
- Loss of a beloved grandparent
- Going off to college

- A breakup or divorce
- Finding a job
- Leaving home
- Experiencing an empty nest
- Growing older and losing strength
- Wondering how your kids are doing
- Visiting a foreign place
- Starting a new career after 10, 20, or 30 years

Those are just a few of the challenging events involved in life. When you actively decide to explore and intimately get to know fear, life becomes much less intimidating. But if you're actively avoiding fear and all things scary—note that I'm not referring to physical danger here, but emotional and psychological fears—life will be one miserable day after another.

When it comes to your emotional wounds and traumas, they can be scary. Generally, the unstated fear is that once the dam breaks, it'll never stop gushing. That's why, as a society, generally, we idolize putting our heads down and bulldozing through life. If you're too busy to slow down, you don't have to think about it.

The problem is that trauma and emotional wounds still unconsciously affect your life and relationships. You think of yourself as a good person, but you deeply hurt someone you love. You see yourself as a strong person, yet in certain situations at work or with your partner, you're timid and too afraid to stand up for yourself. Your self-perception is that of a hardworking go-getter, yet you lie on the couch instead of bringing your dreams to life. None of this is saying you aren't good, strong, or hardworking; rather, it points out that some force inside of you is pulling the strings like a puppet master without your consent.

I pose to you these strings are being pulled by your unhealed emotional wounds and traumas. Even the best of intentions and largest dreams are no match for unaddressed, unconscious psychological wounds. The good thing is that addressing these areas can be simpler than you may imagine.

There are four parts to this mindfulness method:

1. Identify the issue
2. Express the feelings
3. Identify the unhelpful belief
4. Try on a new belief

Let's first go through what each step means. Then, I'll give an example from my own life of having applied each step.

Identify the Issue
Often, something that happens at work or in our relationships will remind us of something that happened as a child. For example, your boss being too busy to be available at work might unconsciously remind you of a parent who was too busy to spend time with you. You're furious at your boss but don't realize that much of your anger is related to something unresolved from your past.

Whatever the triggering situation may be, ask yourself what it reminds you of from your past, seeking to understand the association. It could be a one-time event, e.g., the time I overheard dad verbally abusing mom. Or, it could be an ongoing experience, e.g., every time I didn't know exactly how to do something, mom criticized me.

Express the Feelings
Once you identify the issue, find a healthy way to express your feelings. Whether it's fear, sadness, anger, or something else, there are safe ways to express those feelings. Art, body movement, journaling, and music are just a few ways you can let the feelings flow. Remember, feelings are physiological sensations taking place in the body, and that's why something involving movement and expression works well to discharge them.

Identify the Unhelpful Belief
Emotional wounds and traumas come with unhelpful beliefs that negatively affect your life. As an example, if you saw your dad hit your mom, you might believe that all anger is scary, wrong, and to be avoided. As a result, you don't express your anger in healthy ways and you freeze up if someone does express anger, even in a healthy way. Your belief may be something like, "Feeling anger hurts people. Therefore, at all costs, I must not get angry."

Or, if your mom criticized you every time you needed help, you may believe that not knowing something means you're dumb or stupid. So, you only do things you're good at, never venturing out to try something new and exciting.

So, ask yourself, "What is it that this unaddressed wound has me believing about myself?"

Try on a New Belief
If your old belief was a*ll anger is bad*, try on the new belief of a*nger is bad when inappropriately channeled*, or, a*nger itself is never bad, it's expressing anger in dangerous ways that's bad*.

If your old belief was *I'm stupid and an idiot if I don't know exactly how to do something*, try on the new belief of n*ot knowing something I never took the time to learn is normal, and I'm excited to learn something new*. Or *trying something new means I get to have an exciting experience. Plus, I love learning new things*.

Ask yourself: What new belief will help me grow, expand, and open up new possibilities for my life?

Example
Now, let's put the four parts together in a cohesive example.

I was criticized a lot in my upbringing for normal, human behaviors such as not immediately knowing which light switch controlled which light on a panel of multiple switches, not immediately fitting a tool back into a box and having to take some time to examine the shape to get it in properly, or wanting to wear rubber gloves while washing the dishes (we didn't have a dishwasher until later).

Identify the Issue
In my early twenties, I became aware that I believed I was stupid. There was an ongoing sense of being dumb and an idiot. I noticed this belief came up regularly. I used to fight against it by keeping busy, taking a nap, or doing something else to dis-

tract myself from this thought. However, once I'd had enough, I decided to lean in and explore it.

As I leaned into this sense of being stupid, memories of being criticized arose.

The belief I was stupid was a symptom of the unresolved emotional wound of being criticized by a parent. THE problem was the unresolved wound, while the belief about myself was a symptom of the problem.

I had identified the issue.

Express the Feelings
There was a combination of anger and grief within me about having been harshly criticized for normal human behaviors. Through therapy and group intensives like Core Energetics and Barbara Brennan School of Healing, I expressed the anger in safe ways through yelling and using tennis rackets or half of a swimming noodle on a chair. It sounds a bit crazy, but it's certainly healthier than expressing your anger inwardly toward yourself (depression and self-criticism) or by lashing out at and criticizing another human being. The thing about emotional wounds is that when not consciously expressed and processed in healthy ways, they will be unconsciously expressed in their original form. Meaning, if you were criticized, you'll either internally criticize yourself or outwardly criticize someone else— the original form of criticism remains intact.

Once the feeling of anger had ample opportunity to move out of me, I came into contact with grief. Usually anger is a defense against the more vulnerable feelings of grief. I saw my own innocence—I wasn't stupid, I was a small boy who was dependent on his parents. Physically dependent for food and shelter, yes, but also emotionally and psychologically dependent. It's indeed deeply sad when a small child looks up to his parents—all children look to their parents for validation and love—and that parent is capable only of feeding back harshness and criticism because their own wounds haven't been processed. Parents treat their children in ways that mirror how they think and what they feel about themselves.

I allowed myself to grieve, not attempting to hold the tears back. No self-judgment about grieving. Of course, the goal isn't to experience self-pity. There's a difference between feeling the pure energy of an emotion vs. interpreting it as "poor me." This step isn't about how you have it worse than other people or staying stuck in pitying yourself. It's about giving the pure physiological feeling of grief space to express itself. Feel the pain of grief, don't distract yourself from the true pain through self-pity.

After expressing these feelings, something lightened up. Try walking around for 10 minutes with a 20-lb dumbbell in each hand or one 20-lb med ball in your arms. After 10 minutes, set the weights down. Notice the tension being released? It was like that after letting myself express grief. Except, I didn't know I was carrying the weight around until after I had discharged it.

Identify the Unhelpful Belief
Once the underlying feelings are expressed, it's much easier to explore unhelpful beliefs. The reason it's easier is that discharging the feeling removes the charge, hence the term "discharge." With the charge reduced, you can dig in and explore the situa-

tion further without becoming overwhelmed by intense emotions.

The unhelpful belief I was buying into and basing my life on was: I'm stupid and intellectually inferior. This belief resulted in pursuing careers I didn't want, but because I was stupid, so I told myself, I couldn't possibly have a chance at more exciting opportunities. It prevented me from trying and learning new things. *Write a book?* I could never. *Run a retreat?* No way. *Fix a plumbing problem in the bathroom?* I wouldn't know where to begin. *Get a master's degree?* Not smart enough.

The belief I was stupid and intellectually inferior acted as a fence. I had to stay within the fence; otherwise, I'd be in over my head and wouldn't be able to figure out what to do or how to handle situations outside the fence.

Try on a New Belief
I tried on this belief: Even if I don't know a single thing about a subject, I can learn. Not only that, I can enjoy the process of learning.

I brought the belief to life by putting it into action. When something came up I wanted to do, accomplish, or try, I used mindfulness to remind myself of my new belief. *Okay,* a voice in my head would concede, *I'll try it out.*

I started with smaller things like learning new games. Then, took on challenges like changing the oil in my car (which wasn't nearly as challenging as I imagined it to be). I became invested in this concept of consciously adopting new, encouraging beliefs and tried things requiring long-term commitments like starting a blog or fixing car parts I didn't previously know existed. I got even more into it and spoke at groups without planning the words out in my mind. Next, I wrote my first book and eventually finished a master's degree. The new belief was born, grew, and fully blossomed. That's right—beliefs aren't carved in stone, they're grown, like a tree. The circumstances in my life didn't change until something inside of me changed, specifically, my beliefs. Once those changed through consciously growing new beliefs, external circumstances transformed.

Think of the new and exciting things you can do and experience. How can your life change for the better if you adopted, and grew, new, helpful, self-encouraging beliefs? You've always wanted to ski, so pick a day and book a lesson. Maybe you'll love it and want to go again, or you could hate it and that'll be your first and last time. The adventure is in trying it out. Or maybe you want to learn a foreign language. It's as simple as getting the book and reading three pages per day or listening to five minutes per day on an audiobook. You'll find it's not so much about the time commitment—it's more about the beliefs you have about yourself pertaining to the new thing you want to do. Therefore, change your beliefs to fit the goals you want to achieve. Reread that: Change your beliefs to fit the goals you want to achieve. It's possible because beliefs are *grown*, not flipped on and off like a light switch. Be mindful of when an old belief tries to run the show of your life, pause (if this book is about one thing, it's about pausing), and insert your new belief. Then, take an action that grows the new belief.

Simple Application

Beliefs are attached to unresolved emotional wounds and traumas. Therefore, the next time you notice yourself emotionally escalated, follow these steps:

1. Ask yourself, "What past event or series of events does this remind me of?"

2. Take several minutes to feel and express your emotions regarding the past event(s).

3. Identify the unhelpful belief you hold about yourself, the world, and life in general.

4. Create a belief that encourages you to grow and move toward the life and person you want to be, then grow that belief through new actions.

Mindfulness Method #5

The Panic Attack Paradox

In *Learn to Love Yourself Again*, I discussed a panic attack I experienced as a junior in college. Briefly, the background information is that I was grabbed by the throat as a teenager and developed a vocal cord issue.

As the years went by, the vocal cord problem became worse. By the age of 21, it was nearly a constant issue, meaning it didn't just act up here and there like in previous years, but affected my ability to speak daily. Because I hadn't yet learned to psychologically and emotionally handle speaking "differently" than other people, I was nervous about a speech I'd be giving in front of my Intro to Politics class.

The speech escalated into a full-blown panic attack. It was the first time my voice truly "locked up." The more difficult it was to speak, the more anxious I became. I battled and fought, trying to force the words out. To no avail, my mind desperately sought a solution. *What's happening to me?*

My breathing became shallow and rapid with a skyrocketing heart rate. I felt myself become white as a ghost as my vision became blurry in the periphery. The blurriness became blackness. With the blackness closing in and my line of sight narrowing, it seemed I'd be passing out soon.

Looking back, I wish I'd stopped the speech right there and said, "Something's wrong. I need to go." I didn't have any concept of that level of self-care or even of that being a possibility. Luckily, I stopped and said something like, "Whoa. I feel dizzy." I paused and took a few solid breaths, preventing myself from passing out.

All of that to share this next part, which isn't in *Learn to Love Yourself Again*. Fast forward to the next semester. The main project for my Environmental Physiology class would be a presentation in front of the class. As soon as I heard that, I went into panic mode. I had been sitting in class quietly and comfortably, but now my heart rate was through the roof and my body's muscles were tightening. I was in a panic at the very mention of doing a presentation in front of a class again. I talked with the professor and he allowed me to write a report instead of doing a presentation. *Phew. What a relief.*
Except, not really.

Although it was my best option at the time, as I had no idea how to emotionally and mentally work through this issue, at some point, I'd still have to face the inner dragon. It was either that or spend the rest of my life in avoidance mode.

~ ~ ~

There's a common theme evident in all cases of aggressive anxiety and panic, whether referring to my story, my clients' stories, or your story: Avoidance.

I was doing my best to avoid situations that looked like the one I was in when my panic attack took place. The clients I work with who experience panic start there, too. It's a natural starting place when dealing with this issue. *I want to get away from the panic attack.*

There's a thing about panic and anxiety. A crucial thing. It's something I didn't understand back then but is crystal clear now. The more you avoid, the bigger the dragon grows. It gets bigger, stronger, scarier, and better at hiding out in the shadows and striking when you least expect it. Likely, you react to the "hiding dragon" in two common ways: Premeditated avoidance and in-the-moment avoidance.

Premeditated avoidance is what I did in my Environmental Physiology class. I got ahead of the situation so I wouldn't have to experience it at the end of the semester. But in-the-moment avoidance is what I did during the presentation where I almost passed out. This type of avoidance takes the form of battling and fighting against the feelings of anxiety and panic as they're happening. The anxiety begins and then you bite, scratch, and kick to try and make it stop. Although you're fighting against the anxiety, it's still a form of avoidance because you're trying to make it stop, go away, or otherwise separate yourself from it.

With premeditated avoidance, the dragon becomes more distant and unknown to your conscious mind each time the approach is used. The more distant the dragon becomes, the more afraid you become of it, as we fear what we don't intimately know. (Remember our earlier discussion about fear of the unknown?) Eventually, the fear becomes part of you, which you simply accept as "you." As examples:

I just don't dance.

I don't talk in front of groups.

I'm not big on leaving the house.

What began as premeditated avoidance turns into part of your character, subtly directing your life from the background, much like an app that still eats your phone's battery power even though you didn't realize it was operating in the background.

In-the-moment avoidance happens when you find yourself in a situation you don't want to be in. You might breathe faster and harder. Your mind races. *This will be terrible. Oh my gosh. Stay calm, stay calm, stay calm! Deep breaths, deep breaths. Why isn't any of this working!?*

It can't possibly work because you're fighting against yourself. If you're fighting against you, then you always lose. There's no potential winning scenario. The key is to stop fighting.

~ ~ ~

Today, there are still times I feel anxiety about my voice. This is especially true when I'll be spending time in a group of people I don't know well. When your voice sounds like mine, people get confused. *Is he drunk? Mentally delayed? Sick? Something else wrong with him?* Some people will directly ask why my voice is like that while others won't ask, but their facial expressions say it all.

It's been 18 years, but I remember well what it's like to have a speaking voice that functions normally and effortlessly. I'd go to parties and get-togethers, joining right in the conversation without people making faces, asking questions, or making judgments.

For years, I avoided. Didn't want to go out, talk to people, etc. That didn't work for me because the dragon was still there. If I have to avoid the dragon, that means the dragon is alive and well. It's big, strong, and has power over me. Avoidance wouldn't be necessary if it didn't have power over me. Would you avoid a small fruit fly? Of course not.

After a while, I decided this was no way to live. I have one life— do I really want to live it in avoidance mode?

I eventually found an answer, and it was completely counterintuitive.

~ ~ ~

The only thing that works is embracing, stepping into, and exaggerating the feeling. Remember from Mindfulness Method #2, it's the feeling you're afraid of. I didn't want to be judged, looked at sideways, or have comments made about my voice because of how I'd *feel* about them. The thing I fear—my own feelings—happens inside of me, not outside.

So, what's the approach, exactly? When I'm on my way to a gathering or event, I feel my anxiety as intensely as possible. I exaggerate it. Notice it in my chest, gut, and legs. Let it course through my spine and head. If my throat feels tight, which it often does due to my vocal cord issue, I'll exaggerate the tightness. Try to make it tighter and more constricted. The key is to embrace and welcome the very feelings I fear and want to avoid.

After a minute or two of doing this, I'm excited. Yes, really. Think about it: Why wouldn't I be excited? I've just faced down the thing I'd been fearing and anxietizing about. Having embraced it, it's no longer a fear or point of worry. The dragon isn't hiding in the shadows, waiting to engulf me in fiery flames. The feelings have been processed, dissolved, vaporized.

Feelings simply need to run their life course. By embracing, exaggerating, and intensifying the pure energy of the feeling, not the thought, you can work through your feelings of fear and anxiety before the circumstance which you're associating fear and anxiety with ever takes place.

The key is to focus on the pure energy of the feeling in your body, not your thoughts about the situation. In my situation, thoughts come in the form of imagining images of people's judgmental faces and the rude things they'll say. The feeling I'll feel about that is fear and anxiety. The fear and anxiety are physiological, while the thoughts are images and words in my mind. As the feeling runs its course, you'll notice it in the form of physiological sensations in your heart, gut, throat, head, back, and legs. Once the feeling has completed its course, the thoughts have no power.

This method is indeed counterintuitive and paradoxical. Remember, this book is about *outsmarting* negative thinking. If this book contained only methods that already made sense to you, then working through anxiety and negative thinking wouldn't be a problem. The key is to think outside the box.

The concept sounds wild, I know. I hope you'll keep an open mind. *Why would anybody in their right mind actively seek the thing they're trying to avoid?* I get that train of thought. The distinction you must remember for this mindfulness method to work is that you're not afraid of the situation, you're afraid of the feelings you'll experience. Remember, and this is the pinnacle, those feelings take place inside of you. This is why it's an inner issue, not an external one.

~ ~ ~

As previously mentioned, explaining it like this has helped my clients tremendously: **Anxiety is fear projected into the future**.

Remember when I asked my professor if I could write a report instead of doing a presentation in front of the class? Well, I wasn't afraid of that moment; I was afraid of the future. When I'm feeling anxiety about being judged for my voice, I'm not afraid of that moment. I'm afraid of the future. Therefore, if I can drop the future-based thinking and feel the fear in the now, I can also work through the fear in the now. When you bring the fear into the now instead of projecting it into the future, you might notice your body physically relaxing. This happens because you're no longer fixated on something you can do nothing about—the future. Living in the now is much more pleasant, even if you're working through fear. Without the future, anxiety simply becomes fear in the here and now. I've found addressing the fear head-on in the here and now to be much more effective than ongoingly projecting it into the future and experiencing constant anxiety, tightness, and incessant negative thoughts.

Fear is uncomfortable, sure, but remember from Method #1 that an emotion is just an emotion. Without the thoughts attached to it, it's nothing more than a physiological sensation. You can handle a physiological sensation.

Battling panic and trying to make it go away is like trying to put a fire out by pouring a bucket of lighter fluid on it. Your avoidance and your fighting against the panic fuels the fire. Instead, cut off its oxygen supply, as fire cannot exist without oxygen. Your feelings of fear, not your thoughts, as many believe, are what fan the flame of panic. Allowing your feelings to flow and even exaggerating them at this moment so they run their life course is like quickly sucking out all of the oxygen from a room where a fire is burning.

Once you let yourself feel the uncomfortable feelings in the here and now, viewing them as a natural physiological sensation, you'll find there's no fear remaining to project into the future and feel anxious about.

Simple Application

Take it from someone who would panic every time his voice didn't function properly, which was dozens of times per day: Panic grows and becomes more intense when you try to make it go away.

Instead of swinging for the fences when panic comes up, utilize mindfulness to notice it. Then, take the brave and effective step of welcoming the uncomfortable feeling of panic. You'll discover that panic can only control you when you try to make it go away. As long as you welcome it, you control it.

Mindfulness Method #6

<u>Framing</u>

As I alluded to earlier, when I meet new people, they rarely know how to react to my voice because it sounds so different due to my vocal cords not opening and closing properly.

Even mature adults don't know how to respond, because it's not like anything they've ever heard. We all know what a stutter is, so when we encounter someone with a stutter, we don't react squirmishly. We also understand what a missing limb is, so, hopefully, we don't give a person with a missing limb strange looks or ask them personal, probing questions. When something is unknown to us, however, we often react in unconscious ways because our minds are trying to process and make sense. Unknowingly, you might change your facial expression, drop your jaw, or want to move away because your mind is taken aback by something it doesn't know how to interpret or categorize.

With that in mind, I like to ease the tension with people, especially in professional settings. I'll say something like, *don't worry, I'm not sick, my voice sounds like this from an old neck injury*. Once I say that people's bodies visibly relax because their minds stop running a thousand miles a minute, trying to make sense of the unique voice they're hearing. I use this method to move things forward and get down to business. I have neither the time nor desire to share my life story with every new client or professional colleague, and I've found this tactic to be effective while requiring only a few seconds of my time.

At one job interview, I explained how my voice has been an excellent tool for building rapport with clients. *It seems there is an almost automatic rapport that's created when I tell them about my voice,* I explained. *I suspect it levels the playing field, meaning, while I'm still the skilled professional who is there to support them through the vulnerable parts of their life, I'm also seen as a mutual human being as opposed to an all-knowing authority figure with a shell too thick to be penetrated.*

In explaining this to my interviewer, he responded, "Hey, that's a great reframe!" Here's the thing about reframing: You better believe it, or some part of your mind will know it's fake and, therefore, won't relieve your negative thinking and anxiety. Reframing is about finding truth. It's not about lying to yourself or living in la-la land and acting like problems don't exist. It's about focusing your attention on an interpretation that promotes growth or creates fun as opposed to fixating on something you can do nothing about.

Let's apply reframing to something small, then work up to applying it to more consequential situations.

~ ~ ~

The Wi-Fi went out earlier today. We tried resetting it twice. When that didn't work, we used the data on our phones to find outages in our area. Sure enough, our area was on outage alert. When this happened, I was about to type emails, download reports, and do other work requiring the internet.

I could have fought against the situation. *Who the fu*k is our internet provider? I'm switching providers! I can't believe they won't answer the phone. This is just ridiculous.* Sounds like a fun way to spend an afternoon, right?

Instead, I did the work I could with the data on my phone, then viewed it as an opportunity to read a section of a book I've been curious about. I peacefully dozed off for a few minutes after reading, and I'm now typing this. Nice and energized, I'll be working with clients soon. Was it frustrating that the internet was out? Sure, but focusing on that would've drained my energy and set me off onto a path of negativity for the rest of the day.

On social media, people often post something like, "Don't you hate when you're having a good day and then you spill your food and it ruins the rest of your day? #FML #WhyMe? #ICantCatchABreak"

First, the person who posted that was either rushing from running late or distracted from something else when they spilled their food. Their day was already hanging on by a thread, to begin with. Never have I spilled my food unless I was in a hurry or distracted. Second, spilling your food doesn't need to mean the remainder of your day will suck. It can be the beginning of an *even better* day—the day you outsmart negative thinking for the first time. With reframing, you can view it as a beautiful opportunity to reset yourself after obviously having been rushing or distracted. It's not "the day" that's bad; it's how you frame the experiences of the day that make it pleasant or unpleasant.

To clarify, I'm not saying don't express your frustration. But if you must, do it immediately and move ahead with reframing. (Be careful about expressing anger and frustration in front of toddlers and small children, as they don't have the capacity to process the difference between general anger and anger at them. With that in mind, you might process your anger someplace else, such as in the car, for example.) I might let out a colorful word or two (or seven) when I spill my food. The difference is that I will express my feelings right then and there, followed by resetting and moving forward peacefully. Unlike the me from many years ago, I will not interpret one moment of frustration as meaning my entire day has to be filled with frustration. Negative thinkers are typically rigid, but practicing transitioning from a moment of frustration to a moment of peace improves your mental and emotional adaptability and flexibility.

~ ~ ~

Kicking things up a notch, what's a major issue in your life you wish would just go away? For me, there were many, and I'll choose major depression as an example.

Depression can be debilitating. There was a period in my mid-twenties when I thought about suicide daily and spent my days in bitterness. A personal trainer, I couldn't build a clientele because I called off work so much due to being so low. To leave the depression behind after nine years of living with it, a reframe was necessary.

Now, this wasn't any small reframe—given that depression had found its way into every nook and cranny of my mind, a large shift was necessary. I found there were two primary ways of dealing with depression: 1. The Fix It Approach, and 2. The Growth Approach.

I tried The Fix It Approach first, which involved medication and cognitive behavioral therapy. Helped by medication and some counseling, I felt a bit better. (Keyword: "bit".) I wasn't as miserable or unhappy; however, it seemed that "I" was gone.

I could function and interact with people. I could go to work. But I wasn't there. My body and brain went through the motions, but there was dullness on the inside. Externally functional but internally numb.

The Fix It Approach was the best I had. Was I completely miserable? Nope. Was I happy and fully alive? Also, nope. I will not get into the story of how I discovered The Growth Approach, as that's a topic for an entire book currently being written. For now, I'll summarize it like this: I viewed my depression as a symptom of something deeper needing to be addressed.

The Growth Approach was a rocky road at first, and nowhere close to as creamy as actual Rocky Road ice cream. Eventually, as I continued experimenting with seeing depression as a symptom as opposed to THE problem, I noticed a positive pattern.

Whenever I addressed the problem underlying the feeling of depression, I felt happier and more peaceful. At first, the peace and happiness were short-lived. However, as I continued facing and addressing the *why* beneath the depression, peace and happiness remained for longer periods of time. That's how The Growth Approach works—by interpreting depression as your built-in check engine light which then guides you to address the underlying issue that triggered the light to go on. When the check engine light goes on in your car, you don't just remove the light or put a piece of electrical tape over the light so you can't see it. Instead, you fix the underlying mechanical problem, and the light naturally goes off.

As an example, I had lots of emotionally harmful experiences during childhood. Negative beliefs resulting from the unprocessed emotions associated with these experiences were alive inside of me, but I did my best to act as if I was unaffected by my childhood experiences. Just like storms naturally happen when hot and cold air meet, mental health problems naturally manifest when intense emotions and negative worldviews go unprocessed.

Rather than continue trying to make the symptom go away—in this case, depression was the symptom—I addressed the unprocessed emotions and negative worldviews. I did this through:

- Therapy
- Journaling
- Reading books on whatever problem was coming up at the time
- Working a 12 Step program
- Attending experiential workshops (Gestalt, Core Energetics, Barbara Brennan, Hero's Journey Foundation, Making Peace with Your Past [Middleburg Heights, OH], to name a few)
- Practicing the skill of noticing, as soon as possible, the unhelpful belief or unprocessed emotion coming up
- Asking for help and mentorship from people who used to be where I was but were now in a better place

Reframing the depression as a symptom of a deeper problem rather than THE problem allowed me to view it (the depression) as an ally that pointed me toward what needed to be addressed instead of my enemy. Eventually, the depression was gone. After having addressed the root causes thoroughly enough— unprocessed emotions and negative worldviews—there simply wasn't enough raw material for depression to continue living on inside of me. Remember, this was after nine straight years of living with it. Since we can't physically see depression in the same way we do a flat tire or cracked smartphone screen, we view it as mysterious and ungraspable. In reality, specific conditions must be present for depression to exist. When those conditions are addressed, depression can no longer flourish. By reframing depression as a symptom of those conditions, I gained the confidence to explore what those conditions were and worked through them. For the sake of absolute clarity, those conditions are unprocessed emotional hurts and negative worldviews.

~ ~ ~

The power of reframing lies in its ability to unleash energy, motivation, and encouragement. I view reframing a lot like installing a curtain rod.

You're standing on a step ladder, but the positioning of the ladder is too far away to safely reach where the rod needs to go. You step down, reposition, and now you can safely reach the area where you'll be installing the support hook for the curtain rod. Given the awkward shape of the support hook, you can't just drill it from a straight angle like a screw going into the wall with nothing in the way. You've got to find the proper angle where the hook doesn't hinder your drill, but you can still get a strong push into the screw.

The entire process is going in for a closer look, making an attempt, then stepping back to get a bird's eye view followed by making the appropriate adjustments and trying again. You adjust the ladder and drill angle over and over until you get it where you need it. And, oh yeah, I just did all of that a few minutes ago.

With any situation in life, step back and look at it from the perspective of an observer. When something helpful or useful comes to mind, go back in and try it out. Continue stepping back and taking an onlooker's perspective again and again until you find a way of looking at it or thinking about it that propels you towards growth or resolution.

94

Last, an important point: There are dozens of ways to perceive any given situation. For example, here are eight possible ways to perceive most challenging, stressful, or unideal situations:

1. Nothing ever works out for me. Something always has to go wrong.
2. Maybe I'm not supposed to [fill it in]—I'll take this as a sign to pursue something else.
3. God must be against me.
4. What's wrong with me? I'm such an idiot. I always make huge mistakes. Just once, I'd like to get something right.
5. This person's/organization's operational procedures are ridiculous—I can't stand them.
6. Meh. I'll just stay busy with other things.
7. All my hard work is down the drain.
8. Why me?

Notice that all of the above viewpoints are negative. It's very, *very* easy to come up with a negative, anxiety-ridden viewpoint in nearly any situation. Way too easy. I've come across one explanation of this that says we had to constantly be on the lookout for danger during more primitive times of existence. If we were off our game or unfocused for any period of time, we risked falling prey to a large, hungry animal. Therefore, our brains evolved to be excellent at finding dangers and negatives in any given situation.

Reframing requires the effort of actively seeking a positive perspective, with the key phrase being that you must actively seek the encouraging viewpoint. To be clear, I'm not talking about positive thinking where you ignore all the negatives and move forward with blinders on. This is more about acknowledging that, "*Yes,* there are many potential negative ways of seeing this situation. However, given that my life is not physically in danger in this situation, I'm going to actively seek a positive way of perceiving it."

Simple Application

There's no super-secret to reframing—just follow these simple steps:

1. Step back and take an observer's perspective.

2. Explore various ways to conceptualize the situation.

3. Choose one viewpoint and ask, "Does this perspective promote growth?"

4. If yes, try it out. If no, explore other ways of conceptualizing the situation until you find one that does promote growth.

Mindfulness Method #7

Actively Feed Your Mind

What are you feeding your mind?

We've all heard it, and frankly, most of us think it's pie in the sky.

What am I feeding my mind? My mind doesn't eat, my mouth eats!

I've always had an interest in animals, and at 27 years old, I rented a National Geographic DVD from the library about the animal kingdom. Of course, there was footage of predators and prey. I'll save you the details, as the images disturbed me to the core.

I was so disturbed, in fact, that I called my mentor on the phone. When I told him what I'd watched, he responded, "Don't be watching those types of images—cut that out! Inner healing means healing everything, and that includes the images you're letting into your mind." Well then, Ron, why don't you tell me how you really feel? He was often straight forward with me through the years we worked together. I often felt angry about how direct he was, but now that he's gone, I appreciate it deeply because I see he wanted what was best for me.

In breaking this down, we see I watched some images and then had a sense of being disturbed inwardly. This surprised me, because as a teen and into my early twenties, I could watch that type of thing and it did not affect me. . .so I thought. As it turns out, those were some of the unhealthiest, mentally dysfunctional years of my life.

Consider this concept of feeding your mind in terms of drinking alcohol. Three drinks will affect someone who has never had a drink, whereas three drinks will do little or nothing to someone who drinks regularly. If the regular drinker stops drinking for a couple of years and then has three drinks, they will now be affected by the alcohol. The lesson is that being numb to something doesn't mean it's neutral in terms of your mental and emotional health. Your mind will eventually view whatever you feed it as "normal" if it eats and digests enough of it, but *normal* and *healthy* are not always the same.

Along with disturbing images of horror movies, shows, and videos, the news is a major source of unhealthy food for the mind. Out of the trillions of events that occur each day, ranging from good, neutral, to bad events, the news focuses on the problematic ones. Murder, war, death, and politicians constantly saying and doing the wrong thing from the perspective of whichever particular news channel you prefer. Expose your mind to this for long enough, and you'll surely adopt a fear-based, judgmental outlook.

People often say, "But I want to know what's going on in the world," and while that's a good point, it's only partially true. There are trillions of activities going on in the world, many of which are neutral, good, useful, positive, and helpful. Every day, people are donating to charities, helping someone in need, sharing an uplifting word, and giving a welcoming hug. To watch the news is to decide to focus almost exclusively on the problematic events of the world, which is adopting a lopsided viewpoint. There's a lot of ugly in the world, sure, but there's also a lot of beauty.

Ron once said, "Peace is all around if you'll only open your eyes to look for it." Constant exposure to the news media is certain to result in a stream of negative and anxious thoughts even when you're not watching, reading, or listening to it.

Do you remember the documentary *Supersize Me*? A man ate only McDonald's to understand the effects doing so would have on his body and health. When you're not mindful about what you feed your mind, only exposing yourself to what's fast and easy—which, news media certainly is fast and easy, as you are told what to think, believe, and be afraid of rather than being presented with objective information and then interpreting that information for yourself—your mind loses health and functionality like the *Supersize Me* man's body lost health and functionality.

You may not notice any adverse effects while your mind takes in the unhealthy food, but the result is a lopsided worldview, clouding your ability to experience peace, joy, excitement, and happiness. It's a subtle poison, which is the most dangerous kind because you don't realize it's gradually compromising you.

In the section about framing, you learned that how to gauge how to reframe any given situation in your mind is by asking yourself, "Is this perspective in some way promoting growth, peace, or wellness?" This can be easily adapted to evaluating what you feed your mind. Ask yourself, "Is what I'm feeding my mind promoting inner peace and happiness?"

For me, watching images of predators and prey was not. Similarly, most people I know who immerse themselves in news media outlets are constantly angry, anxious, or upset about something. Therefore, ensure whatever you feed your mind passes the litmus test of promoting your well-being before ingesting it.

~ ~ ~

We've discussed the harm of feeding your mind unhealthy foods. Now, let's look at the benefit of feeding your mind healthy foods.

It's much easier to let your mind be filled with negativity. If it weren't, a book such as this wouldn't be needed. Remember, mindfulness means stopping to evaluate what's happening. Mindfulness, and therefore outsmarting negative thinking, is only possible when you pause to evaluate. Initially, pausing might seem like a mighty halting of a 10-ton bus. As you practice pausing, it becomes more like stopping and going on a casual walk. You stop to admire wildflowers here, go again, then stop to take in a stream over there. Just as noticing nature is part of a casual walk, so, too, will pausing to evaluate your thought processes become part of your character.

Feeding your mind healthy foods means ingesting materials that motivate, inspire, heal, promote growth, or create inner peace. For example, I like to stop throughout the day and take in the trees outside. Their greenness, lushness, and the way they sway back and forth is good for my mind and soul. There's a green tree frog living inside a pillar that supports our back porch, and watching him brings a sense of happiness at the beauty of nature. (I know it's a "him" because I researched green tree frog sounds. The species apparently thrives in Louisiana.) There's also a hawk that will land on a fence in our neighborhood. It flies away shortly thereafter, landing only to briefly check out the scene, but seeing it for just a few seconds gives me a sense of awe. These things don't take long—even a few seconds to a minute feeds your mind with something healthy.

Other, more obvious examples include inspiring or growth, promoting podcasts, videos, and documentaries. Oh, and books. Reading or listening to a book that directly counteracts negativity and fills your mind with encouragement, positivity, growth, and the ability to work through obstacles is an excellent food source to regularly ingest. Yes, I'm aware that saying, "Hey, you! Read books!" sounds silly because:

a) It's generic. Telling someone to read a book has been done and overdone. And

b)   You are literally reading a book right now.

Given the seeming ridiculousness of such a claim, I'm either a ridiculous person OR I have a really good reason for exploring this. And the answer is . . .

Both.

I am a ridiculous person. There's no doubt about it. Additionally, I have a good reason for exploring this.

Have you ever thought about why reading is so helpful? Learning new things, blah blah blah, and all of that, yeah. However, for outsmarting negative thinking, there's a more specific reason it's so important.

Anxiety is a major underlying driving factor of negative thinking. You see how they're interrelated, right? Anxiety feeds negative thoughts and negative thoughts feed anxiety. For many people, this cycle is continuous throughout life. But learning new information and understanding a subject *relieves* anxiety. To prove it, here are two examples:

First, our bathroom sink broke a few months ago (props to me for that one). I was flustered and frustrated, along with all the other unpleasant moods. I'd never done any plumbing work, so the entire setup—sink, pipes, joints, and so on—was interpreted by my mind as one big and confusing conglomerate of a mess.

After being insane in the membrane (and, props to Cypress Hill for that zesty phrase) for a while, I took a closer look, studying where and how the pieces connected and watching videos that explained the inner workings, which couldn't be figured out by just looking. Soon, I had learned new information that transformed the sink setup from a confusing conglomerate into a clear, coherent system.

What changed? The sink and pipes surely didn't change by magically turning into Legos I could click into place. What changed was that my mind had ingested new information. That new information made the situation intelligible. As humans, things we don't understand can be frustrating and scary . . . but we're not nearly as afraid of those same exact things once we gain new information about them.

As a second example, the same concept of learning new information applied to my experience of major depression. I was utterly terrified of depression. It seemed there was nothing I could do to get over it. It was like an invisible monster that could do whatever it wanted to me because I couldn't see, touch, or understand it.

A mentor, Dan, recommended I see a therapist, Ron, who lived in Erie, PA. (Ron has been mentioned several times already.) One way, Erie was 90 minutes from Cleveland, Ohio, which is where I lived. Because of the distance, I resisted going. Dan encouraged me to see Ron for about a year. When I couldn't seem to find any way of hiding from, blocking out, or medicating my depression, I finally made the drive to see Ron.

Ron taught me about how depression works. I asked questions and he gave answers. He recommended books, I read them, thus learning new information. The more I worked with Ron and the more I read his book recommendations, the more understanding I had of depression. Eventually, I understood how it worked and what exactly I could do about it (a forthcoming book in this series). For the time being, the point is that even depression, as terrifying and mysterious as it was to me, when better understood through ingesting new information, lost its sense of scariness and frustration.

Again, I'll ask this same important question: What changed? Certainly, the depression itself didn't change by suddenly deciding to go easy on me. What changed was my perception of it. I could go on and on with stories of situations that were initially frustrating and scary but became neutral or even fun and exciting once new information was gained, but two is enough to drive the point home.

The new information you gain from a book changes how you perceive your challenge, thus removing fear and frustration. So, yes, "read books" is a common and generic recommendation, but, when applied, one that effectively reduces anxiety.

~ ~ ~

To summarize, be mindful of what you're feeding your mind. Is it promoting growth, peace, or joy? In our society, it's easy to feed your mind with foods that create fear and anger, but it takes a conscious effort to feed your mind with healthy materials. Taking a moment to look at the sky, an animal, or a plant can do wonders for you. My experience has been that even 20 seconds of this can offset an hour or more of frustration. And remember, feeding your mind with materials that improve your understanding of the challenges and stress points you're facing will wipe away fear, frustration, and anxiety.

Simple Application

Beware of remaining on autopilot, never considering whether what you're ingesting is building you up or bringing you down. Instead, consciously choose what goes into your mind.

Summary
and
Parting Note

To outsmart negative thinking, mindfulness is the key. Are you caught up in the whirlwind of your thoughts and feelings, or are you pausing to observe them? Observing frees you to choose how to handle your thoughts and feelings, whereas being caught up in them means *they will handle you*. By stepping back to observe your thoughts and feelings, you're empowering yourself to have a choice in determining which mindfulness method to use.

"An emotion is just an emotion" sounds obvious, almost to the point of being silly, but we interpret emotions as meaning something negative. It's okay to experience feelings of anger, grief, and fear. When you feel them in your body, interpreting them simply as a "physiological experience," instead of attaching negative meaning to them, you'll truly see that an emotion is nothing to be concerned about.

It's possible you may not know what you're really afraid of. Do you need to take a moment to figure it out? Many people believe they're afraid of a person or situation when, in fact, the situation poses no physical threat. Instead, the threat is emotional and psychological. Fear of being rejected, told "no," judged, or turned down is fear of your *own feelings*, not of a person or event. Identify the feelings you're afraid of within yourself, then work through those as opposed to fixating on the outer object of your fear.

Evaluating this moment, right here and now, can be useful. Is there an immediate issue or danger present you can do something about right now? If yes, take action. Are you in an environment that's peaceful, aside from the thoughts racing through your mind? You'll need to remind yourself that all is well at this particular moment.

Facing your trauma and emotional wounds head-on might sound ridiculous. After all, you may have based your life around avoiding these areas. But when not faced head-on, they control you from a place below your conscious awareness. Squarely addressing these areas affords you the opportunity to discharge them from your body. It also provides the ability to try on fresh, helpful beliefs that will get you where you want to go as opposed to the old beliefs holding you back.

The Panic Attack Paradox works for panic in addition to general anxiety. Fighting your fear equals fueling the panic or anxiety, whereas embracing it equals diminishing the panic or anxiety. Panic happens when you try to make the fear go away, but can't. Instead of continuing to battle the fear, turn the idea that you have to get away from the fear upside down and inside out by embracing the fear. You'll be pleasantly surprised.

Will you take the angle of framing? There are dozens of ways you can interpret any given situation. Seeing a situation so it promotes growth, fun, or excitement will keep negative thinking from overtaking your mind.

You may need to reevaluate what you're feeding your mind because what goes into your mind will manifest into thoughts and feelings. Are you consciously choosing what goes into your mind or going along with the status quo? It's okay to turn the news off. You're allowed to unfollow people on social media whose content you don't like. Yes, even friends and people you respect. Seek life-giving, growth-promoting materials that will mentally and emotionally nourish you. Try reading an inspiring poem. Get a motivating book or audiobook. Do or watch something lighthearted. Look at some wildflowers. The important thing is this: Are you consciously choosing what goes into your mind?

As a parting note, these methods will work best the earlier you can implement them in the negative thinking cycle. That's why mindfulness is the pinnacle, because it allows you to detect negative thinking early, before it snowballs into a full-blown avalanche. Don't fear, because the methods will still work even if you use them after negative thoughts have gained some momentum. Remember, however, that it's much easier to snuff out a golf ball-sized snowball than a boulder-sized snowball. Don't forget the downloadable gift at the beginning of this book—it will act both as a reminder to remain mindful and supply the tools you need for outsmarting negative thinking.

You can do this. No matter how bad your negative thinking is right now, you can experience happiness. My negative thinking was so bad over a decade ago that I regularly called in sick to work, lost clients, and even considered killing myself for a period of time. I'm so glad I stuck with the inner healing process, as it's how I learned the methods in this book, which I now have had the honor of passing along to you.

One Last Thing

Did you know that a review from you makes a huge difference? It's true.

It makes a difference in the lives of others. Most people choose books based on reviews, so if another human being is in need of learning these mindfulness methods, leaving your review helps them understand how this book can bring them hope and encouragement.

We've all had the experience of buying a life-changing book based on the review of a person who we'll never meet.

With reviews, just one single sentence describing what you gained from this book is more than enough, and it can be completed in less than 60 seconds. It's easy—simply go to the product page of this book and scroll down until you see a button that says "Write a customer review". Click the button, and from there, it's a user-friendly, fast, and easy process.

Get in Touch

There are a few ways to get in touch:

Join my email list at www.nicsaluppo.com and receive the eBook *The Five Laws of Emotional Resilience* as a bonus when you join.

Email me at nicsaluppo@gmail.com.

Find me on Instagram at the handle @nicsaluppo.

Next Book in the Series

Mental Health Crusader
Storm Your Mind and Take Back Your Mental Health

When it comes to mental health challenges, who's really the enemy?

Is it negative thoughts? How about painful emotions like sadness, anxiety, or anger? Is the enemy your beliefs about yourself? On all fronts, the answer is a resounding *no*.

To be a victorious mental health crusader, you must accurately identify what you're fighting against. Carl Jung put it well when he said, "Wholeness is not achieved by cutting off a portion of one's being, but by integration of the contraries."

In our society, we think the answer to our mental health problems is to "snuff out" the negative portions of our being. This leads us in never ending circles and greater and greater frustration. The answer is to win the battle against the true enemy, Divisiveness.

When you're divided within yourself, you can't achieve stable mental health. Learn to be victorious in the crusade against Divisiveness so you can begin to experience inner peace.

Mental Health Crusader is available on Amazon.